AI for Beginners

Learn What AI Is, What It Can Do for You, and
How to Start Using It - Even If You're Not
Tech-Savvy

Angus David

Table of Contents:

Introduction

You've probably heard it a hundred times:

"AI is the future."

"It's going to change everything."

"If you don't learn how to use it, you'll be left behind."

Maybe that excited you. Maybe it overwhelmed you. Maybe it just made you close the tab.

Here's the truth: most people feel a mix of curiosity and confusion when it comes to AI. They're interested, but unsure. They hear the buzz, but don't quite know where to start — or whether they even belong in the conversation.

This book is for those people. If that's you, welcome. You're not late. You're not behind. And you absolutely don't need to be a tech expert to begin.

Why This Book Exists

The goal of this book is simple: to help you understand what AI is, what it can actually do, and how to start using it — even if you've never touched a chatbot in your life.

This is not a book about coding, data science, or engineering. It's not about building AI. It's about using it.

Specifically, it's about using it in everyday ways — to write, plan, learn, explore, and think more clearly. Whether you want to save time at work, organize your thoughts, boost your creativity, or just stay curious about how things are changing, this book will show you how.

And more importantly, it'll show you that **you can do this** — without having to become someone you're not.

What You'll Learn

This book will take you from *I don't really get what AI is* to *I'm using it in ways that actually help me*.

You'll learn:

- What AI is (in plain English)

- How tools like ChatGPT and others actually work behind the scenes

- How to ask better questions and get more useful answers

- Where AI can support your work, creativity, and daily life

- What to watch out for — and how to use these tools responsibly

- Where to go next if you want to go deeper

Along the way, you'll see real examples, practical prompts, and simple explanations — no jargon, no tech-speak, no pressure.

You don't need to read it all in one sitting. You can move at your own pace, skip around, or just read the chapters that interest you most.

Who This Is For

This book is for beginners. That means:

- You're new to AI, or have only dabbled with it

- You've heard of tools like ChatGPT, but aren't sure what to do with them

- You want to start using AI without being overwhelmed by technical detail

- You're not looking to build AI — you're looking to benefit from it

If you've already been using AI tools every day and you're deep into automation, prompting strategies, or building workflows, this book might feel like a warm-up. But if you're still figuring out what a "prompt" even is, you're in exactly the right place.

What This Book Isn't

This isn't a hype piece. It's not about selling you the promise of AI, or warning you about dystopian futures. It's also not a manual. You won't need a whiteboard, a headset, or a glossary of terms.

This is a guide — written to be read like a conversation. A way in. A step forward. Something you can hold in your hands and say, *Okay. This makes sense now.*

What You'll Need

To get started, you'll need:

- A basic internet connection

- An open mind

- A willingness to try things out (even if they feel weird at first)

You don't need to be tech-savvy. You don't need to be confident. You just need to be willing to take the first step — and let this book walk you through the rest.

Because AI isn't some exclusive club or secret language. It's a tool. One that's already shaping the world — and one that's now in your hands, ready to support your voice, your goals, and your ideas.

Let's begin.

What Is AI, Really?

Demystifying Artificial Intelligence

What AI is (in plain language)

Artificial Intelligence, or AI, is a branch of computer science that focuses on building systems capable of performing tasks that would normally require human intelligence. These tasks include things like understanding language, recognizing images, solving problems, learning from experience, and making decisions.

In simple terms, AI is when a computer is trained to "think" in a limited, specific way — not like a human with emotions or creativity, but more like a tool that can analyze information and produce useful responses, often faster and more accurately than a person. It doesn't mean the machine is alive or conscious. It just means it's been given the ability to follow patterns, process data, and generate results based on what it has learned.

Right now, the most common AI tools are used to help people write, summarize, translate, generate images, answer questions, or organize ideas — often through natural, conversational interfaces. Think of AI as a powerful assistant that can help you do things more efficiently, without needing deep technical knowledge to use it.

The difference between AI, machine learning, and automation

These three terms are often used interchangeably, but they mean different things — and understanding the distinction will help you feel less overwhelmed.

Artificial Intelligence (AI) is the broadest term. It refers to the overall concept of machines doing tasks that typically require human intelligence. That could mean understanding speech, making decisions, generating text or images, or recognizing patterns.

Machine Learning (ML) is a subset of AI. It's one of the main ways modern AI systems are created. Instead of being programmed with a long list of rules, machine learning systems "learn" from data. You feed the system many examples — like thousands of cat photos — and it figures out for itself what makes a cat a cat. The more data it sees, the better it gets.

Automation is a separate but related concept. It refers to using technology to carry out repetitive tasks with little or no human involvement. Automation doesn't necessarily involve intelligence. For example, setting up your email to sort messages into folders is automation. If an AI tool learns your habits and sorts your emails based on patterns — that's automation powered by AI.

In short:

- **AI** is the umbrella concept.

- **Machine learning** is how many AI systems learn.

- **Automation** is what many AI tools help us achieve more efficiently.

Why "thinking robots" is a myth (and what's actually true)

Thanks to movies and TV shows, a lot of people imagine AI as a super-intelligent robot with emotions, a personality, and the ability to make independent decisions — like something out of *The Terminator* or *Iron Man*. But in real life, AI isn't anything like that.

AI doesn't **think** or **feel** the way humans do. It doesn't have opinions, desires, or self-awareness. It doesn't "want" anything. It can't be creative or original in the human sense. What it does is follow instructions and patterns based on data it has seen before. It can generate results that *look* impressive — like writing an article, answering questions, or creating an image — but it's not doing that because it understands the world. It's doing it because it has learned what combinations of words or images are likely to make sense based on everything it was trained on.

Imagine a super-powered parrot with a gigantic memory: it doesn't know what it's saying, but it's really good at repeating things in clever ways. That's closer to what AI is right now.

So, no — we're not living in a future of robots that think for themselves. Today's AI is more like a helpful tool that follows smart instructions and mimics certain skills, without truly understanding what it's doing.

A Brief History of AI

How we got here: key breakthroughs and timelines

Artificial Intelligence might feel like a brand-new trend, but the idea has actually been around for decades — even centuries, in some form. People have long dreamed of creating machines that could think, speak, or act like humans.

Here's a quick look at the key moments that brought AI from science fiction to everyday reality:

1950s – The Idea Takes Shape: British mathematician Alan Turing posed the question: *Can machines think?* He introduced the concept of the "Turing Test" — a way to judge whether a machine could convincingly mimic human conversation. Around the same time, researchers began experimenting with early AI concepts.

1956 – The Term 'Artificial Intelligence' Is Born: A group of scientists met at a summer workshop at Dartmouth College and officially coined the term "artificial intelligence." They believed that machines could one day replicate human reasoning. This event is often considered the birth of AI as a field.

1960s–1980s – Early Hype and Early Struggles: In these decades, researchers built early AI programs, including systems that could play chess or solve math problems. But AI didn't live up to the hype, and funding dried up. These slow periods are sometimes called the "AI winters."

1997 – Machine Beats Human at Chess: IBM's Deep Blue defeated world chess champion Garry Kasparov. It was a huge milestone and proof that computers could outperform humans in very specific tasks — but only when programmed with enough data and rules.

2010s – Machine Learning Rises: The big shift came when computers became powerful enough to learn from data — not just follow rules. This gave rise to machine learning and deep learning, which power many of today's AI systems.

2020s – AI Becomes Mainstream: AI tools that generate text, images, video, and even music have become widely available. These tools are trained on massive amounts of data and can now help people write emails, create artwork, analyze data, and more — all without needing any programming knowledge.

In short, AI didn't appear overnight. It's the result of decades of breakthroughs, setbacks, and slow-building progress. What changed recently is that AI has become much more accessible — and that's why you're hearing about it everywhere now.

The Rise of Consumer-Level AI Tools

For most of its history, AI was something only scientists, engineers, or big tech companies worked with. It lived in labs, universities, and behind-the-scenes in business systems. Ordinary people had no direct interaction with it — and often no idea it was even there.

That all changed in the last few years.

Thanks to advances in computing power, access to huge amounts of data, and smarter algorithms, AI tools have become faster, cheaper, and easier to use. Now, everyday people — not just developers or researchers — can use AI in simple, powerful ways.

Here's how consumer-level AI exploded into the mainstream:

AI Got a Friendly Face: Instead of complicated code or robotic interfaces, AI tools now talk to you in plain language. You can type a question or a command — like "summarize this paragraph" or "create a dinner plan for two" — and get instant results. That shift from code to conversation made AI accessible to everyone.

The Tools Became Web-Based (and Free): You no longer need to download special software or learn a new system. Many AI tools are available right in your browser — free or low-cost — and take minutes to try. This "zero barrier to entry" opened the floodgates.

Real Results Made People Pay Attention: Once people saw AI writing emails, creating images, drafting business plans, or helping with schoolwork — they realized it wasn't just a novelty. It was useful. That usefulness spread through word-of-mouth, social media, and news stories — and suddenly, AI was everywhere.

Today, there are AI tools for writing, drawing, designing, scheduling, learning, brainstorming, researching, and more — all designed for beginners to use without any technical background. This is a key moment in tech history, because for the first time, powerful AI is no longer behind locked doors. It's in your pocket, your browser, and your everyday tools.

Why AI Is Suddenly Everywhere Now

It might feel like AI exploded out of nowhere — one day it was a buzzword, and the next, it was writing emails, generating art, passing exams, and even showing up in job descriptions.

So, what changed? Why is AI suddenly part of every conversation, news headline, and business tool?

Here are the key reasons:

The Technology Finally Caught Up: For years, AI was limited by slow computers and small datasets. Today, we have powerful cloud computing, faster processors, and enormous amounts of data — all of which make AI faster, smarter, and more useful. It's not that AI suddenly appeared — it's that it finally works well enough to impress and help everyday users.

The Tools Got Easier to Use: A major shift happened when AI tools stopped requiring technical knowledge. You no longer need to code or configure anything. Instead, you can interact with AI using everyday language — just type what you want, and the AI responds. That simplicity removed the fear and made AI feel approachable.

Mass Adoption Created a Snowball Effect: Once millions of people started sharing what AI could do — whether on social media, in the workplace, or at home — others got curious. Businesses started integrating AI into their tools. Educators began teaching with it. Creatives explored it. That collective excitement made AI go from niche to normal almost overnight.

In short, AI is everywhere now because it became **powerful**, **easy**, and **visible** — all at the same time. And that's why so many people (maybe you included) are now wondering: *What is this, really? Can I use it? Where do I even begin?*

This book exists to help you answer those questions — clearly, calmly, and without the overwhelm.

Why AI Matters to You

Real-Life Problems AI Is Already Solving

AI might sound like a high-tech concept, but its value becomes obvious when you see how it solves **real problems** — the kind you might deal with every day.

Here are just a few examples of what AI is already helping people with:

Saving Time on Repetitive Tasks: AI tools can write summaries, generate reports, organize information, or even draft emails — things that normally eat up hours of your day. Instead of starting from scratch, AI gives you a starting point (or sometimes a finished product) in seconds.

Helping with Decision-Making: From suggesting the fastest route on your GPS to offering recommendations for movies, books, or products — AI is constantly helping you make quicker, more informed choices. It's behind the scenes, but it's making everyday life smoother.

Making Life More Accessible: AI-powered tools can transcribe speech for the hearing-impaired, read text out loud for those with vision difficulties, or translate between languages in real time. This kind of assistance is opening doors for millions of people who were previously limited by barriers in communication or access.

Improving Customer Service: Many companies now use AI-powered chatbots to answer customer questions instantly. These bots can handle simple issues — like checking order status or resetting passwords — without needing to wait on hold or talk to a human rep.

Supporting Creativity and Learning: Whether you're trying to write a blog post, brainstorm product names, learn a new language, or design a logo — AI tools can assist by offering suggestions, generating ideas, or even creating drafts you can refine.

In short, AI isn't just a tech trend — it's a **useful tool that solves everyday problems**. It's already woven into your daily life in ways you may not have noticed. And once you start using it intentionally, you'll likely wonder how you ever managed without it.

The Growing Role of AI in Work, Creativity, and Life

AI isn't just showing up in a few apps — it's quickly becoming part of how we **work, create,** and **solve everyday problems**. Whether you realize it or not, AI is already shaping the world around you, and its role is only expanding.

Here's how it's beginning to touch nearly every area of life:

In the Workplace: AI is helping people write reports, manage schedules, draft presentations, and even analyze data. In marketing, it generates social media captions and blog ideas. In HR, it helps sort through job applications. And in customer service, it responds to common questions 24/7. It's not about replacing jobs — it's about removing the boring, repetitive parts so people can focus on higher-value work.

In Creative Projects: Writers are using AI to overcome writer's block. Artists are experimenting with AI-generated imagery. Musicians are composing with the help of AI tools. Entrepreneurs are using AI to develop product ideas, slogans, or business names. Even if you're not an "artist," AI can help bring your ideas to life faster and easier than ever.

In Everyday Life: AI is becoming your quiet assistant — helping you plan meals, draft emails, organize your calendar, track habits, learn new skills, and even reflect through journaling prompts. It's not just a work tool — it's a **life tool**, helping you manage your mental load and make better use of your time.

The key point is this: **you don't have to be a tech expert to benefit**. The role of AI is no longer just for software engineers and big companies — it's for freelancers, parents, teachers, students, small business owners, and curious beginners. In other words: people like you.

Why Now Is the Best Time to Start Learning

There's never been a better time to learn about AI — and more importantly, to start using it. You don't need to wait until you "know more," and you don't need to worry about being behind. In fact, you're stepping in at exactly the right moment.

Here's why:

AI Is Still New for Everyone: Despite how it may look online, most people are still figuring this out. The tools are new, the rules are evolving, and best practices are still being discovered. You're not late — you're early. Getting started now means you can grow with the technology instead of playing catch-up later.

The Tools Are Easier Than Ever: AI has never been more user-friendly. Most tools are designed for everyday people, not programmers. They're free or low-cost, and they don't require any technical skills. You can experiment, learn, and improve at your own pace.

Early Adopters Will Have the Advantage: Whether you're thinking about your career, your business, or your creative projects, those who learn how to work with AI will have a serious edge. It's not about replacing people — it's about **enhancing your abilities**. Knowing how to use AI effectively could help you get hired, grow faster, save time, or simply get more done with less stress.

AI is here, and it's not going away. But that's not something to fear — it's something to **explore**. And the sooner you begin, the more confidently and creatively you'll be able to use it in your own life.

This book is your guide to doing exactly that.

Common Myths and Misunderstandings

Busting the "AI Is Too Complicated" Belief

Why You Don't Need to Be Technical to Use AI

One of the biggest things that holds people back from trying AI is the idea that you need to be "good with computers" to understand or use it. But that's simply not true anymore.

Today's AI tools are designed for **real people** — not programmers, not engineers, not tech experts. If you can type a sentence into a search bar or send a text message, you already have the skills you need to start using AI.

Here's why you don't need to be technical:

AI Has a Simple Interface: Most AI tools today work just like a chat window. You type something in — a question, a request, an idea — and the AI responds. It's like talking to a very smart assistant who's always available. No coding, no setup, no manuals.

You Don't Have to Know How It Works to Use It: You probably don't know exactly how your microwave or your smartphone works, but you still use them confidently. AI is the same. You don't need to understand the algorithms behind it — just what it can do for you and how to give it good instructions.

Mistakes Are Part of the Process: The truth is, even the most experienced users make mistakes or get strange results from AI sometimes. That's normal. The key is to approach it with a mindset of play and curiosity — test things out, try new ideas, and learn by doing.

You don't need to be "technical" — you just need to be **willing**. If you can bring your curiosity, this book will help you with the rest.

What AI Can't Do (Yet)

While AI is incredibly useful and growing more powerful every year, it still has clear limitations — especially when compared to how humans think, feel, and operate in the real world. Understanding what AI **can't** do helps you use it more effectively and avoid expecting too much from it too soon.

Here are some important boundaries to be aware of:

It Doesn't Truly Understand Meaning: AI doesn't actually "get" what you're saying. It recognizes patterns in words and phrases, then responds based on what it has seen in its training data. If you give it a vague question or something with emotional nuance, it may give an answer that sounds right but misses the point entirely.

It Can Be Confidently Wrong: AI generates responses by predicting what sounds correct — not by verifying facts. This means it can produce information that's outdated, biased, or just plain incorrect. It's smart to double-check anything important or factual, because AI doesn't have a built-in sense of truth or accuracy.

It Doesn't Think or Feel Like a Human: AI can come up with ideas or creative outputs, but it doesn't have instincts, emotions, or lived experience. It doesn't *care* about what it's producing — it's simply generating possibilities based on patterns. It can be a great creative partner, but the emotional depth or originality behind the work still comes from you.

It Isn't General Intelligence (Yet): There's a concept called **Artificial General Intelligence (AGI)** — the idea of a machine that can think, learn, and adapt like a human across many areas of life. AGI would be flexible, independent, and capable of reasoning on its own. But today's AI is still narrow and task-specific. It can do one thing really well — like write a paragraph or recognize a photo — but it doesn't understand the world or itself.

So, while AI might feel advanced — and in many ways, it is — it's still just a tool. A powerful, exciting tool, yes. But not a thinking mind. Not yet.

Separating Hype from Reality

With all the headlines and viral claims floating around, it's easy to feel overwhelmed by what AI might be — or fear what it might become. But to move forward with confidence, it's important to separate what's real from what's exaggerated.

First, let's be honest: AI can do some impressive things. Watching it write an article, generate an image, or organize your ideas in seconds really can feel like magic. But it's not magic — it's pattern recognition at scale. That means it still gets things wrong, and it doesn't actually *understand* what it's doing.

"AI is a great helper, not a perfect genius."

You've probably heard people say that AI will take over all jobs. The reality? **AI is more likely to change jobs than eliminate them.** It's excellent at handling repetitive, rule-based tasks — like summarizing notes or sorting information. But it still relies on humans to guide it, shape its output, and make final decisions.

Now, let's talk about those jaw-dropping results you see online — the flawless essays, mind-blowing images, instant marketing plans. What you don't usually see is the *editing, prompt tweaking,* and *trial and error* it took to get there. In the real world, **you'll still need to be involved** — even if AI gives you a head start.

So yes, AI is powerful. And yes, it's going to reshape how we live and work.

But don't believe the hype that says it can do *everything,* or that it's going to leave everyone behind. **The truth is this:** the people who benefit most from AI will be the ones who *learn to use it thoughtfully* — not the ones waiting for it to do all the thinking for them.

"AI Will Take Over Everything" – Not Quite

The Difference Between Replacement and Augmentation

One of the biggest fears people have about AI is that it's going to replace them — take their job, their role, or their usefulness. And while it's true that AI is shaking up how many industries operate, the idea that it will "take over everything" misses an important distinction.

AI doesn't have to replace people — it can *augment* them.

Let's break that down.

Replacement is what happens when a job or task is fully handed over to a machine, with little or no need for human involvement. Think of a factory robot welding car parts. The machine does the same thing, every time, often faster and more efficiently than a person.

But *augmentation* is different. It means the technology helps you — making your work faster, easier, or more effective, while **still needing your input, ideas, or judgment**.

Imagine this:
You're writing an article. AI can help you generate an outline, suggest titles, or even draft a few paragraphs. But it's still you who shapes the tone, adds your unique voice, checks the facts, and makes sure it says what you really mean. That's not replacement. That's teamwork.

Here's another example:

A customer service rep uses an AI tool that suggests replies or highlights the customer's tone. It speeds things up — but the rep still decides what to send, how to say it, and when to take a different approach. **The person stays in control.**

Think of AI as your power tool — not your replacement. It speeds things up, but it doesn't do the job *for* you. It still needs your hands on the handle.

In short, the biggest opportunity isn't about AI doing everything. It's about **you + AI** doing things better — together.

How AI Is Creating New Kinds of Jobs

Whenever a big new technology shows up, it's normal to worry about what might be lost. And yes — some tasks that used to take hours can now be done in minutes with AI. But history shows us something important: when technology changes how we work, it usually creates **new kinds of work**, too.

The same is happening with AI.

Here are just a few examples of jobs and roles that are either emerging or growing because of AI:

1. Prompt Writers and AI Content Designers: These are people who specialize in knowing *how* to talk to AI tools — giving clear instructions, refining outputs, and getting the best possible results. Just like good writing or design, crafting the right AI prompt is a skill. And companies are hiring for it.

2. AI Assistants and Workflow Optimizers: As more teams adopt AI tools, they need people who understand how to fit those tools into daily workflows. These aren't programmers — they're practical thinkers who can spot ways to save time, reduce repetition, or improve output using AI.

3. Human Reviewers and Editors: AI can generate text, images, or insights — but it still needs a human to check for accuracy, tone, and context. From copy editors to fact-checkers, this "human-in-the-loop" role is becoming more important as AI output increases.

And then there are the ripple effects — businesses that never had content teams now have one-person marketing departments thanks to AI. Freelancers are able to offer faster services. Creatives are turning ideas into products without needing large teams.

The key takeaway: AI won't just change *what* we do — it's already changing *what's possible*. And the people who learn to work with it are finding new ways to create value in the world.

So, instead of thinking only about what jobs might vanish, ask this: **What could I do — or create — if AI handled the boring parts?**

Ethical Concerns, Explained Simply

As AI becomes more powerful and more widely used, it brings along some big questions — not just about what it *can* do, but about what it *should* do. You don't need to be a tech expert to understand these concerns. They're about fairness, truth, privacy, and responsibility — things that affect everyone.

Let's look at a few key areas in plain, human terms.

Bias in the Machine: AI tools learn by studying examples — usually millions of pieces of text, images, or conversations pulled from the internet. But the internet isn't neutral. It reflects all kinds of human biases: racial, gender, cultural, and more. That means AI can sometimes give answers that repeat or even amplify those biases, even when no one intended it to. It's a known issue, and while researchers are working on it, it's still something to watch out for.

Real or Fake? It's Getting Harder to Tell: One of the challenges with AI is how easy it is to create things that look real — realistic photos, articles, voices, or videos. This opens the door to misinformation, fraud, and deepfakes. If anyone can generate a believable-looking news story or image in seconds, how do we know what to trust? That's a big question society is now grappling with.

Your Data, Your Control: Many people don't realize that AI systems are trained on huge datasets — and sometimes that includes public content created by regular people. This raises questions about consent, ownership, and privacy. Plus, when you use AI tools, your input might be stored or used to improve the system. It's important to know what a tool does with your data — and to be cautious about sharing anything personal, sensitive, or private.

That doesn't mean you should be afraid to use AI. It means you should use it **with awareness**.

The more you understand the risks, the better choices you can make — for yourself, your work, and the communities you're part of.

Addressing Fear and Hesitation

Tech Anxiety Is Normal — and Solvable

If you feel nervous, overwhelmed, or even a bit embarrassed about not understanding AI, you're not alone. In fact, it's more common than you might think.

Many people — smart, capable people — feel behind or hesitant when faced with new technology. They might think:

> *"What if I mess it up?"*
> *"Is it too late to learn this?"*
> *"I'm just not good with tech."*

Here's the truth: **you don't have to be naturally "techy" to learn how to use AI.** You just need the right environment — one that makes space for curiosity, patience, and a few mistakes along the way.

Think of it like learning to drive. At first, you might feel awkward, unsure, even a little intimidated. But with some guidance and low-pressure practice, it starts to feel natural. AI is similar. You're not expected to know everything from the start. The key is just to start.

A few gentle reminders that help:

- Everyone starts as a beginner — even the experts you see online.

- Confidence grows through **doing**, not just reading or watching.

- It's okay to explore AI at your own pace, in your own way.

Don't let fear of "not knowing enough" stop you. What matters most is your **willingness to try** — and this book is here to guide you one step at a time.

You Don't Need to Understand Everything to Get Started

One of the biggest roadblocks for beginners is the belief that they have to "get it all" before they begin using AI — that they need to fully understand how it works under the hood before they're allowed to touch the tools.

But that's simply not true.

Think about how you use everyday technology: You likely don't know how your smartphone processes data, how your Wi-Fi router handles packets, or how your car's engine manages combustion. And yet — you use them all the time. Why? Because they're designed to work *with you*, not depend on your technical expertise.

AI is becoming the same way. The best tools today are built so that anyone — including complete beginners — can jump in and start exploring without needing to understand the inner mechanics.

Here's what really matters when you're starting out:

- Knowing **what's possible**

- Learning **how to give clear instructions**

- Getting comfortable **experimenting and adjusting**

You can learn everything else along the way. Understanding the basics will help, sure — and this book gives you that foundation. But don't wait until you feel "ready." You'll learn faster (and with more confidence) by doing.

Start small. Stay curious. Use what you learn. That's how real progress begins.

Building a Positive Mindset Toward AI

Your mindset shapes how you experience new things — and when it comes to AI, the right mindset can make all the difference.

It's easy to get stuck in fear-based thinking: *"What if I break it?"* or *"This isn't for people like me."* But AI isn't some exclusive club for tech insiders — it's a tool. And tools are meant to be used by real people with real needs.

Rather than thinking, *"I have to master this,"* try shifting your thinking to: **"I'm allowed to learn as I go."** This one change can unlock the freedom to explore without pressure.

A few mindset shifts that help:

- **From fear of failure → to freedom to explore.** Mistakes aren't signs you're doing it wrong — they're part of how you learn what works.

- **From "I'm behind" → to "I'm early."** Most people are still figuring this out. Starting now means you're ahead of the curve, not behind it.

- **From "I don't belong in this space" → to "AI is for people like me."** You don't need permission. If you're curious, you're ready.

AI isn't something to conquer — it's something to **grow into**, piece by piece.

You'll make progress. You'll get better. And as you do, you'll realize that the biggest barrier was never the tech itself — it was just the story you were telling yourself about it.

How AI Works (Without the Jargon)

The Basics of AI Systems

Inputs, Outputs, and How AI Makes Decisions

Let's break down what happens when you use an AI tool — in the simplest way possible.

Imagine you're asking an AI assistant to help you write a birthday message. You type in: *"Write a short, funny birthday message for my best friend."*

That's your **input** — the instruction or request you give the AI.

The tool reads your input, analyzes it, and produces a result — maybe something like: *"Happy Birthday! You're now officially too old to blame your bad decisions on youth. Congrats!"*

That's the **output** — the AI's response based on what you asked.

But how did it go from your message to that reply? Here's the basic idea:

1. **It looks at your input** and breaks it into keywords and patterns it understands.

2. **It searches its training data** — all the examples and patterns it learned from — to find the most likely kinds of responses.

3. **It generates an answer** by predicting the next best word, one piece at a time, until it completes the response.

It doesn't "understand" your birthday request like a person would — but it's good at guessing what a helpful or funny answer might look like, based on all the examples it's seen before.

So, in short:

- You give the AI **input** (a question, task, or command)

- It processes that using patterns it has learned

- It returns an **output** — often quickly, and usually impressively

Understanding this basic input/output loop will help you use AI tools more effectively. The clearer your input, the better your results.

Understanding Prompts, Models, and Data

If you've spent any time around people who use AI tools, you've probably heard words like *prompt*, *model*, or *training data*. These can sound intimidating at first, but they're actually quite simple when broken down.

Let's take a look.

Prompts: Talking to the AI - A *prompt* is just the message or request you give to an AI tool — it's how you "talk" to it.

- Asking it to write something: *"Summarize this article in 3 bullet points."*

- Giving it a role to play: *"Pretend you're a fitness coach and create a 10-minute home workout."*

- Requesting something creative: *"Write a haiku about coffee."*

Think of prompts as instructions — the better and clearer they are, the better the AI's responses will be. You don't need to be a programmer to write a good prompt — just be specific and direct.

Models: The Brain of the AI (Sort of)

The *model* is the engine that runs under the hood. It's the part of the AI that was trained to understand language, patterns, and tasks. Models are built by feeding huge amounts of information into a system until it can recognize how things usually work.

Different models have different specialties. Some are good at writing. Others might focus on generating images, translating languages, or recognizing speech. When you use an AI tool, you're using a model that was trained to do that kind of task.

You don't need to know the model's name or the code behind it — just that it's the "brain" that takes your prompt and produces an answer.

Training Data: Where the Learning Comes From

Before AI can do anything, it needs to learn — and that happens through *training data*. This is the information the model studied to understand how language works, how images are built, or how conversations flow.

For example:

- A language model might be trained on books, websites, news articles, and online conversations.

- An image model might be trained on thousands or millions of labeled pictures.

This data gives the AI a foundation to "guess" what a reasonable response or result would be when you give it a prompt.

You don't need to memorize any of this — just remember:

Prompt = what you ask

Model = the system that responds

Data = the examples it learned from

These three pieces work together to produce the results you see — often in just a few seconds.

Why AI Needs Training — and What That Means

AI doesn't come out of the box knowing anything. It has to be trained — and that training is what gives it the ability to respond to your questions, understand language, or generate useful results.

But don't picture a classroom or a teacher. AI learns in a very different way.

Training an AI means feeding it enormous amounts of data — sometimes billions of words, images, or examples — and allowing the system to find patterns, connections, and structures in that data.

Let's say you wanted to train a language AI to write restaurant reviews. You'd feed it thousands (or millions) of real reviews so it could learn:

- How reviews are structured

- What kinds of words people use

- The difference between a good review and a bad one

It doesn't memorize the exact reviews. Instead, it notices what kinds of sentences tend to follow each other, which words are used in different situations, and how tone and context shift.

Over time, the system adjusts itself to make better and better predictions — like which word should come next in a sentence, or what kind of response fits a certain type of prompt. This is called **machine learning** — the AI improves based on the feedback it gets during training.

Now, here's the key takeaway: Once the training is finished, the AI tool is *frozen* — it doesn't continue learning from your inputs unless it's specifically designed to do so (and most consumer tools don't). That means it can give impressively accurate answers in many situations — but it doesn't learn from your individual use of it in real time.

In simple terms: AI is trained by studying tons of examples — and once trained, it's ready to generate new things based on what it learned.

Understanding this gives you an edge: when you know AI is working with patterns from past data (not real-time thinking), you're better equipped to guide it, catch errors, and use it wisely.

Types of AI You'll Encounter

Generative AI vs. Predictive AI

As you start exploring different AI tools, you'll notice they don't all do the same thing. Some help you **create** things — like text, images, or music. Others are more focused on **predicting** outcomes — like what product a customer is most likely to buy or which email you're likely to open.

These differences fall broadly into two categories: **generative AI** and **predictive AI**.

Generative AI: The Creator

Generative AI is what most people are excited about right now. These are the tools that *generate* new content based on your input.

Ask it to write a story — it writes one.

Ask it to draw a picture — it creates one.

Ask it to compose a melody — it gives you music.

It doesn't copy and paste from existing content. Instead, it creates something new, based on patterns it learned during training. The results often feel surprisingly human — and sometimes even creative.

You've probably already seen examples of this: tools that write social media captions, design logos, draft emails, or generate photorealistic images from a sentence.

In short: You give it an idea, and it gives you something back that didn't exist before.

Predictive AI: The Forecaster

Predictive AI works a little differently. Instead of creating something new, it uses patterns from past data to make educated guesses about what might happen next.

For example:

It might predict which customers are likely to cancel a subscription.

It might suggest what product you're most likely to click on.

It could recommend what movie you'd enjoy next, based on your past choices.

You've already used predictive AI if you've ever:

Seen a suggested video on YouTube

Gotten an auto-complete while texting

Used a GPS that reroutes based on traffic patterns

Predictive AI is all about probability — looking at what usually happens, and guessing what's likely to happen next.

Which One Will You Use?

In everyday life, you'll probably encounter **both** types of AI —
sometimes without even realizing it. When you use a writing tool,
that's generative AI. When your calendar suggests a meeting time,
that's predictive AI.

As you become more familiar with these tools, you'll start to
recognize which kind of AI is doing the work — and how to use it
to your advantage.

Text-Based AI vs. Image, Video, and Speech Tools

AI doesn't just work with written words — it can also generate
images, audio, and even video. But if you're just getting started, it's
helpful to understand what kinds of tools are out there and what
they're actually used for.

Let's break it down with **real examples** you can explore yourself.

Text-Based AI: Your Virtual Wordsmith

These tools are designed to understand and generate language. You give them a prompt (a question, command, or idea), and they reply in full sentences, stories, summaries, or suggestions.

Popular examples include:

- **ChatGPT** – Conversational writing, brainstorming, summarizing, and more.

- **Claude** – A helpful assistant by Anthropic known for polite, clear responses.

- **Grok** – Elon Musk's chatbot integrated into X (formerly Twitter), with a snarkier personality.

- **Google Gemini** – Integrated into Google products for writing, explaining, and search.

- **Microsoft Copilot** – Built into Word, Excel, and Outlook for help with writing, summarizing, and organizing content.

Used for: Writing emails, blog posts, lesson plans, social captions, summaries, and outlines — or just chatting and learning new things.

Image AI: From Words to Pictures

Image generation tools let you type a description, and they turn it into a visual. They're especially popular with artists, designers, marketers, and content creators.

Popular examples include:

- **DALL·E** – Built by OpenAI (and now inside ChatGPT) for creative illustrations.

- **Midjourney** – Known for artistic, detailed images (popular with designers).

- **Stable Diffusion** – Open-source and highly customizable.

- **Adobe Firefly** – Built into Photoshop and Illustrator for pro-level creatives.

- **Canva AI Tools** – Simple image generation inside the popular design platform.

Used for: Creating book covers, social media graphics, concept art, website visuals, product mockups, and more.

Video AI: Making Motion from Prompts

Video tools are newer and still evolving, but they're gaining ground quickly. Some can animate characters or avatars. Others can create cinematic clips from just a few words.

Popular examples include:

- **Runway ML** – Great for AI-generated video, green screen effects, and editing.

- **Pika** – Create short animated clips from text prompts.

- **Kling AI (by Kuaishou)** – High-quality cinematic video generation from text.

- **Synthesia** – Turn text into talking avatars (popular for training or explainer videos).

- **HeyGen** – AI presenters for business and marketing videos.

Used for: Explainer videos, TikToks, training content, short films, or bringing visual ideas to life without cameras or editing skills.

Speech & Audio AI: Voices and Sounds on Demand

AI can also create human-sounding speech, transcribe audio, or even mimic voices. Some tools are surprisingly lifelike — and they're getting more natural all the time.

Popular examples include:

- **ElevenLabs** – High-quality AI voices that sound realistic and expressive.

- **Descript** – Combines transcription, podcast editing, and voice cloning.

- **Murf AI** – Voiceovers for videos, e-learning, and ads.

- **Speechify** – Converts text to speech for listening on the go.

- **Whisper (by OpenAI)** – Accurate speech-to-text transcription.

Used for: Creating narration, turning blogs into podcasts, editing voice recordings, or making audio content more accessible.

How to Choose?

If you're just starting out, stick with what feels useful:

- **Writing and planning?** Try ChatGPT or Claude.

- **Visual content?** Try Midjourney or Canva's AI features.

- **Audio or podcasting?** Explore Descript or ElevenLabs.

- **Making video content?** Test out Runway or Pika.

You don't have to master everything — just pick one area, try a tool, and build confidence from there.

Rule-Based vs. Learning-Based Systems

Not all AI systems are built the same way. Some follow strict instructions. Others adapt and "learn" from data. Understanding the difference helps you spot what kind of AI you're dealing with — and what to expect from it.

Let's break it down simply.

Rule-Based Systems: If X, Then Y

Rule-based AI follows a fixed set of instructions. Think of it like a very advanced flowchart. If you give it Input A, it gives you Response B — every time. It can only do what it's been explicitly told to do.

You've probably used rule-based systems if you've ever:

- Interacted with a basic customer service chatbot that only responds to specific keywords

- Used a menu system that says "Press 1 for billing, Press 2 for technical support"

- Played an old-school video game where enemies always move in the same pattern

These systems are predictable and safe — but limited. They don't adapt to new situations or learn from experience.

Learning-Based Systems: Pattern Finders

Learning-based AI (like ChatGPT, Claude, or Midjourney) works differently. Instead of following a rigid set of rules, it learns from **massive amounts of data**. It finds patterns in language, visuals, or behavior and uses those patterns to generate a response that fits your input.

For example:

If thousands of people ask for a meal plan, the AI starts to recognize what a "good" one looks like — and it can build a new one on the fly.

If it sees how users typically respond to "write a friendly email," it can predict the tone and structure that fits that request.

This kind of AI is more flexible and creative — but also more unpredictable. It may surprise you (in good or bad ways), and it can make mistakes. It doesn't follow a script — it responds in real time, based on what it has "learned" from past examples.

Which One Are You Using?

Most modern consumer AI tools — especially those that generate text, images, or audio — are learning-based. They've been trained on massive datasets and can respond in ways that feel conversational or creative.

But you'll still run into rule-based systems too — especially in older tools or simpler use cases like:

Smart home routines

Basic phone menu systems

Pre-scripted customer service bots

As a user, it helps to know:

Rule-based = predictable but rigid

Learning-based = flexible but needs clearer guidance

Knowing what's under the hood can help you tailor your expectations — and get better results from any AI system you use.

Everyday Examples of AI at Work

AI in Your Smartphone (And You Didn't Notice)

You might think AI only lives in futuristic tools or fancy software — but the truth is, **you've probably been using it every day without even realizing it.** One of the best examples? Your smartphone.

Today's phones are packed with tiny AI systems quietly working behind the scenes to make your life easier, smoother, and more personalized. You're not just carrying a phone — you're carrying a pocket-sized bundle of machine learning.

Here are just a few ways AI is already at work on your device:

Typing and Autocorrect: When your phone suggests the next word in a text, fixes your spelling, or changes "teh" to "the" — that's AI. It's learned from millions of writing patterns to predict what you're likely to say next.

Voice Assistants: Siri, Google Assistant, Alexa (on Echo devices), and others all use AI to understand your voice, interpret your requests, and give you spoken responses — whether you're asking for the weather, setting a timer, or sending a message.

Face and Fingerprint Recognition: Unlocking your phone with your face or fingerprint? That's AI-powered too. These systems recognize patterns unique to *you*, learning to identify you accurately while protecting your data.

Photo Organization and Enhancement: Your photo app often uses AI to sort images by location, people, or events. It might even suggest "Best of the Month" highlights or remove background blur from a selfie. Some phones can now even enhance blurry photos using AI sharpening tools.

Smart Replies and Email Suggestions: When your email app suggests a quick reply like "Sounds good!" or "Let's do it," that's a small AI feature making things faster. It's learned from typical responses and patterns to offer you time-saving shortcuts.

These aren't flashy tools — they're quiet, helpful, and built into the apps and systems you already use. The more you notice them, the more you'll realize: **you've been using AI all along.**

Recommendation Engines (Netflix, Amazon, YouTube)

Have you ever logged into Netflix and felt like it *magically knew* what show you were in the mood for?

Or noticed how Amazon always seems to suggest something you might actually want to buy?

That's not a coincidence. It's AI — specifically, a kind called a **recommendation engine** — working in the background.

These systems track your behavior (what you watch, click, search for, or buy), compare it with millions of other users' habits, and then predict what you're most likely to enjoy or need next.

Let's look at a few everyday examples:

Netflix or Disney+: When you finish a series and it immediately lines up a similar one, that's AI analyzing:

- What you've watched

- How long you watched it

- What other users with similar taste enjoyed

It then recommends shows or films that align with your past choices — sometimes introducing you to new genres or content you might not have tried otherwise.

Amazon and Online Shopping: When you view a product and see "Customers who bought this also bought..." — that's predictive AI. It's learning from shopping patterns to suggest add-ons, alternatives, or items frequently purchased together.

It also adapts over time. The more you browse or buy, the more tailored the recommendations become.

YouTube and Social Platforms: Ever notice how quickly YouTube adjusts to your interests? After just a few searches or clicks, your homepage fills up with videos on that topic. That's an AI-driven feedback loop — tracking your views, likes, comments, and watch time to surface more of what keeps you engaged.

The same kind of system powers your TikTok For You Page or the suggested posts on Instagram.

These recommendation engines don't just save you time — they shape your experience. They influence what you see, buy, and consume, often without you realizing how customized it's become.

That's the power of AI in action — predicting what you want before you even know you want it.

Smart Assistants and Voice Tools

You might think talking to your phone or smart speaker is just a cool convenience — but behind that simple "Hey Siri" or "Alexa, what's the weather?" is a powerful AI system doing a lot of fast thinking.

Smart assistants like **Siri**, **Alexa**, **Google Assistant**, and **Bixby** use AI to understand spoken language, interpret what you're asking, and deliver useful, real-time responses — often in just seconds.

Let's look at what's happening behind the scenes, and how you're already benefiting from it.

Understanding Natural Language

One of the biggest breakthroughs in AI has been something called **natural language processing (NLP)** — the ability for machines to understand everyday human speech.

When you ask, *"What's the weather like this weekend?"*, the AI has to:

- Turn your speech into text (speech recognition)

- Figure out your intent (are you asking for a forecast, a recommendation, or making small talk?)

- Pull relevant data (based on your location and dates)

- Give you a human-sounding reply

It all happens so fast; you probably don't think twice — but that's AI doing the heavy lifting.

Voice Commands in Daily Life

Beyond answering questions, smart assistants can help with:

- Setting alarms and reminders

- Creating shopping lists

- Controlling smart home devices (lights, thermostats, etc.)

- Sending texts or placing calls

- Playing music, podcasts, or audiobooks

- Giving step-by-step directions while you drive or walk

Some assistants even adapt to your preferences over time — learning your routines, recognizing your voice, and giving more personalized results.

Other Voice Tools You Might Be Using

Even outside of traditional assistants, voice AI shows up in:

- **Voice typing** (on phones or Google Docs)

- **Customer service bots** that let you speak your issue instead of pressing numbers

- **Hands-free search** — like "Hey Google, find coffee near me"

These tools are becoming more natural, more accurate, and more helpful every year.

So, while smart assistants might feel like fun extras, they're actually one of the most familiar — and fast-improving — ways AI is already integrated into your everyday routine.

What AI Can Do for You

Saving Time and Automating Tasks

Drafting Content, Summaries, and Emails

One of the most immediate and practical benefits of using AI is how much time it can save you — especially when it comes to writing.

Whether you're crafting a long report, a quick email, or a list of ideas, AI can take the heavy lifting off your plate by giving you a solid starting point. It's not about replacing your voice — it's about helping you get started faster, with less stress.

Let's look at a few real-world ways it can help:

1. Writing Emails (Without the Blank Page Struggle)

You know that moment when you stare at your inbox, unsure how to word a response? AI can help you get moving by suggesting a draft based on your input.

For example:

> Type: *"Write a polite follow-up email to a client who hasn't replied in 5 days."*

And you'll get a professional message you can tweak and send.

It's great for:

> Customer service

> Sales outreach

Scheduling and coordination

Saying "no" gracefully

2. Summarizing Long Documents or Articles

Instead of reading through pages of text, AI can give you a clear, concise summary in seconds.

Use it to:

Quickly digest reports or research papers

Summarize meeting notes or transcripts

Get the key points from a long article without skimming for half an hour

This is especially useful if you process a lot of information daily but don't have the time to read everything in full.

3. Drafting Content for Blogs, Posts, or Presentations

AI tools can help you brainstorm ideas, generate outlines, or even write rough drafts for:

- Blog articles

- LinkedIn posts

- Newsletters

- Slide presentations

- Social media captions

You're still in charge of tone, accuracy, and final edits — but instead of starting from zero, you begin with a helpful rough version to build on.

Think of AI as your first draft assistant — fast, tireless, and never short on ideas.

Even if you never use its output exactly as-is, it can save hours by sparking ideas and reducing mental load.

Organizing Schedules or Lists

Life can get messy — appointments, to-do lists, grocery runs, reminders, and that one thing you keep forgetting until it's too late. Fortunately, AI can help you stay organized without adding more to your mental load.

Whether you're planning your week, prepping for a trip, or just trying to remember what you were supposed to do today, AI can help you sort it out quickly and clearly.

1. To-Do Lists Made Easy

Instead of spending time figuring out how to structure your list, you can simply tell an AI tool what you need to get done, and it will organize your thoughts into neat, categorized checklists.

For example:

"Create a daily to-do list for a freelance writer juggling two client projects, errands, and exercise."

You'll get something like:

- **Work Tasks**

  Write blog post draft for Client A

  Edit social captions for Client B

- **Personal**

  Grocery shopping

  30-minute workout

- **Reminders**

  Call vet

  Pay invoice

2. Scheduling and Planning

If you have a rough idea of your day but need help mapping it out, AI can do that too. You might say:

"Help me plan a schedule from 9am to 5pm with time for work, lunch, and short breaks."

It'll return a clean outline that balances productivity and rest. This is especially helpful if your days tend to blur together and you need a structure to follow.

AI can also help:

- Plan weekly meal prep schedules

- Build study or revision timetables

- Organize travel itineraries

3. Prioritizing Tasks

When you're overwhelmed with too much to do, AI can help you sort it by priority.

Try:

"Here's a list of 10 things I need to do today — which ones should come first based on urgency and energy level?"

It can help you break big tasks into manageable chunks and recommend the best order to tackle them — reducing the mental effort of decision-making.

The result? Less juggling in your head, and more clarity on paper (or screen).

AI becomes like a virtual planner — always ready, always organized, and never annoyed when you change your mind.

Automating Repetitive or Admin-Heavy Tasks

If you've ever thought, *"There has to be a faster way to do this,"* — AI can probably help.

Many of the small, boring, time-consuming tasks that eat up your day can now be **automated** or **streamlined** with the help of AI. These are things that don't require deep thinking, but still need to get done — like filling out forms, organizing files, or updating spreadsheets.

1. Generating Reports or Data Summaries

If you work with numbers, feedback, or written input — AI can save hours by summarizing or formatting it for you.

For example:

- Turn survey results into a digestible summary
- Convert sales data into a short weekly report
- Reformat customer feedback into clear categories

You give it the raw info; it gives you something polished and ready to use.

2. Automating Customer Replies or Admin Responses

Many professionals are now using AI to handle repetitive communication, especially in areas like:

- Answering FAQs
- Creating polite replies for customer inquiries
- Writing appointment confirmations or follow-ups
- Generating standard invoice or payment messages

You can create templates or use AI to generate slightly varied responses so they still feel human.

3. Document Handling and Filing

Some tools (especially when paired with other apps) can help:

- Rename, sort, or categorize digital files

- Transcribe meetings or video calls into text

- Auto-fill documents like contracts or intake forms

- Extract key info from long documents

Think of it as a **smart assistant** quietly working behind the scenes — not glamorous, but hugely valuable in freeing up your mental space.

You don't need a full-blown automation system or tech team. Many AI tools work with apps you already use — like email, docs, calendars, or spreadsheets.

Start with one repetitive task you hate doing. Ask: **"Could AI help me do this faster, or take it off my plate entirely?"**

Chances are, the answer is yes.

Boosting Creativity and Productivity

Brainstorming Ideas with AI

One of the most helpful ways AI can boost your creativity is by simply **giving you ideas when you don't know where to start.** You don't need to be an artist, writer, or entrepreneur. Everyone gets stuck sometimes — and AI can help unstick you.

Let's say you're trying to:

- Plan a birthday party but don't have a theme

- Figure out meals for the week

- Come up with a gift idea for someone hard to shop for

- Choose a name for your new pet, small business, or even your Wi-Fi network

- Find fun things to do on a rainy weekend with your kids

You can ask an AI tool something as simple as:

"Give me 5 fun weekend ideas for staying indoors with kids."
"What are some unique birthday themes for a 9-year-old who loves animals?"
"Suggest easy meals I can make this week with chicken and rice."

And just like that, it gives you a list of ideas.

Why It's Useful (Even if You're Not "Creative")

You don't need to be creative to use AI for brainstorming. In fact, **you don't even need to know what you're looking for** — you just need a rough idea or question, and the AI helps you shape it into something useful.

It works well because it's been trained on millions of examples — from recipes and party plans to travel tips, names, lists, and more. That means it can pull from a huge knowledge base you don't have to search through yourself.

Try It for Yourself

Here are a few beginner-friendly things you might try:

"Help me come up with five new dinner ideas that don't involve pasta."

"I want to organize my garage — give me a plan to get started."

"Suggest some creative names for my sourdough starter."

"I need a hobby I can do in 30 minutes a day — any ideas?"

No pressure. No expectations. Just a bit of help when your brain feels blank.

AI is like a friendly brainstorming buddy — it doesn't judge your questions, and it never runs out of suggestions.

Experimenting with Music and Sound

Want to make your own relaxing background music? Curious about how lyrics are written? Just want to create a custom ringtone?

You don't need instruments, music theory, or fancy software anymore. **AI can now help you create music, lyrics, and even full vocal tracks — just by typing a few words.** Whether you're just curious or want to explore sound creatively, there's a tool for you.

What AI Music Tools Can Do for You

Depending on the tool, you can:

- Generate instrumental background music

- Write lyrics based on a theme, emotion, or style

- Create entire songs — with vocals, melodies, and beats

- Narrate text in a realistic voice using speech AI

- Remix or isolate parts of existing tracks

Beginner-Friendly Tools to Try

If you're new to music creation, these tools are a great place to start:

- **Boomy** – Make original songs in minutes. Choose a genre, tweak a few settings, and let the AI do the rest.

- **Soundraw** – Great for making instrumental background tracks for focus, relaxation, or content.

- **AIVA** – Compose orchestral or cinematic-style music by setting a mood and letting the AI handle the arrangement.

- **LALAL.AI** – Split songs into vocals and instrumentals. Perfect for karaoke, remixes, or learning how tracks are built.

- **Lyrics tools** – Use **ChatGPT** or **LyricStudio** to generate song lyrics based on a prompt like "Write a song about new beginnings in the style of Taylor Swift."

Cutting-Edge Tools That Use Text Prompts

Some of the newest and most exciting music tools let you create **entire songs — including vocals — by simply describing what you want in words.**

Just like with text or image AI, you enter a short prompt, and the system turns it into sound.

- **Udio** – Type something like *"a lo-fi song about rainy afternoons and coffee"* and Udio generates a full track with vocals and music.

- **Suno** – Similar in concept, Suno creates catchy, high-energy, or emotional songs with AI-written lyrics and realistic vocals.

- **Riffusion** – Originally known for turning spectrograms into music, Riffusion now lets you generate complete songs from text prompts — just like Udio and Suno.

These tools are incredibly beginner-friendly: no instruments, no recording software, no prior experience. Just type, click, and listen.

What Can You Use AI Music For?

- Create calming background music for focus or sleep

- Make silly songs for birthdays or inside jokes

- Add music to videos, slideshows, or personal projects

- Write lyrics to express how you feel

- Try something completely new, just for fun

AI makes music playful again — no pressure, no perfection, just possibilities.

Speeding Up Workflows

You probably have tasks that take longer than you'd like — especially when it comes to writing, sorting information, or pulling scattered thoughts together.

That's where AI can give you a real boost.

It's like having an assistant who's great at **organizing, rewording, and tidying up** whatever you throw at it — fast.

Turning Messy Notes into Something Usable

If you've ever looked at a pile of handwritten notes or a document full of half-formed thoughts and thought, *"Now what?"* — AI can help turn that mess into something clean and structured.

You might try:

"Here's a bunch of notes I jotted down. Can you clean this up into a clear summary?" "Take these bullet points and turn them into short paragraphs." "Organize these ideas into a list with headings."

It's a great way to go from brain-dump to ready-to-use — especially when you're short on time.

Helping with Presentations and Basic Visual Structure

You don't need to be a designer or PowerPoint wizard. AI can help outline slides, suggest visuals, or rephrase long explanations into short bullet points.

You could say:

"I'm giving a short talk about staying focused — help me outline 5 slides."
"Turn this text into a simple slide with a title and 3 key points."

Some tools can even generate full presentation drafts, which you can then adjust to suit your style.

Restructuring Ideas for Clarity

Got a rough idea for a blog post, email, or guide — but not sure how to structure it?

Try asking:

"Organize these ideas into a logical order."
"Turn this into a how-to guide."
"Make this easier to follow for someone new to the topic."

AI can help reshape what you've already written — without you having to rewrite everything from scratch.

Shortcuts That Save Mental Energy

Sometimes the biggest time-saver is not having to think about the small stuff. You can ask AI to:

- Reword something to make it sound more friendly or professional

- Write product descriptions or bios from a few notes

- Suggest quicker ways to explain something

- Edit long texts down to the essentials

You're still in charge — AI just gets you there faster, with less frustration.

Whether you're writing, organizing, or preparing something to share, AI can help you speed things up without cutting corners. It's like moving from walking to cycling — same path, just faster and less effort.

Supporting Personal and Professional Growth

Learning New Skills Faster with AI

One of the most powerful ways to use AI — and one of the most overlooked — is as a personal learning companion. Whether you want to learn a new language, pick up a new hobby, or understand a complex topic, AI can help you **get started faster and stay on track**.

You don't need to sign up for a course or dig through search results. You can just ask, and AI will guide you — step by step.

Start with a Simple Question

Let's say you want to learn something new but don't know where to begin. You could ask AI:

"Explain the basics of photography to a complete beginner."
"Teach me how to meditate in 5 simple steps."
"How do I start learning Spanish from scratch?"
"What are the core concepts of budgeting and saving money?"

AI can break big topics into small, manageable pieces — like a friendly tutor who meets you at your level and gives you just what you need to start.

Learn at Your Own Pace

You can control the pace, depth, and focus. If something feels too advanced, just ask:

"Can you explain that more simply?"
"Give me an example I can relate to."
"Turn this into a beginner-friendly checklist."

AI won't rush you. It won't judge you. And it's available 24/7, which makes it perfect for learning whenever inspiration strikes.

Practice, Review, and Build Confidence

AI can also help with:

Flashcards – *"Create 10 flashcards for basic cooking terms."*

Quizzes – *"Give me a short quiz to test what I've learned."*

Practice exercises – *"Ask me 5 simple questions to practice present tense verbs in French."*

Feedback – *"Here's my paragraph. Can you suggest improvements?"*

Instead of just reading or watching, you're actively *engaging* with what you're learning — and that makes it stick.

Whether you're brushing up on a skill for work or exploring something personal for fun, AI gives you a low-pressure way to move from curious to confident — without needing a teacher, textbook, or strict schedule.

And as you explore more, you'll probably find yourself asking questions you wouldn't have thought to Google — because AI makes it easier to just *ask* and learn. That brings us to another quiet superpower of AI: helping you get clear, direct answers without the usual information overload.

AI as a Tutor or Study Companion

Once you've seen how AI can help you pick up a new skill, it's a small step to start using it as a personal tutor — someone (or something) that's always available to explain things, test your knowledge, and support your learning style.

Unlike traditional study methods that rely on fixed lessons or one-size-fits-all content, AI can respond to you in real time — adjusting to your pace, helping with tricky topics, and even quizzing you when you're ready to review.

Explain It to Me Like I'm... Me

The real magic of using AI as a tutor is how you can say:

"Explain this like I'm a complete beginner."
"Break this down into five short steps."

"Can you reword this in simpler terms?"
"Give me a real-life example of how this works."

And it will adapt — instantly. You don't have to feel embarrassed for not understanding something. You just ask again, and it tries another approach.

That kind of personalized, judgment-free support is what makes AI different from searching for explanations online or watching a generic video.

Study Help That Fits Your Style

Whether you're:

- Reviewing for a test

- Learning a professional skill

- Studying for fun

- Homeschooling your kids

- Or just trying to *finally understand* something that's always confused you

AI can help you:

- Turn notes into summaries

- Create flashcards

- Quiz yourself with multiple choice questions

- Practice explaining a topic out loud (with AI offering feedback)

- Organize topics into a study plan

It's especially helpful for spaced repetition (revisiting information over time to make it stick), breaking big ideas into smaller parts, and helping you track what you know — and what still needs work.

And because it's available anytime — no appointments, no logins, no pressure — it's there when your curiosity sparks, or when you just need a quick confidence boost before a test or meeting.

Learning isn't just about having the right materials — it's about having the right mindset and the right support. And with AI, that support is always a sentence away.

Research and Data Analysis Simplified

Digging through information can be overwhelming — whether you're comparing options, collecting notes, or trying to understand a complex topic. Search engines give you links. AI, on the other hand, gives you *answers* — and more importantly, it helps you make sense of them.

Whether you're planning a trip, researching a purchase, studying for a course, or working on a personal project, AI can save you time and mental energy.

Start by Asking, Not Searching

You don't need to craft perfect search terms or scan 10 different tabs. Just ask a question the way you'd naturally say it:

"What's the difference between plant-based and keto diets?"
"Summarize the pros and cons of switching to solar energy."

"Compare the top three budgeting apps for beginners."
"What are the key points of this article?"

AI can give you a summary, a side-by-side comparison, or a plain-English breakdown in seconds — without information overload.

Turn Messy Notes Into Useful Insights

Already gathered a pile of notes, links, or survey responses? AI can help you:

- Extract key points

- Summarize big themes

- Rephrase data into clearer language

- Organize content into categories or sections

- Turn long info dumps into short, shareable summaries

Even if you're not "good with data," AI helps you feel in control of it. It simplifies the thinking and makes the next step obvious.

Use It for Smarter Decision-Making

If you're choosing between options — tools, plans, purchases, strategies — AI can help by:

- Listing pros and cons

- Highlighting differences

- Asking follow-up questions to narrow your focus

- Giving suggestions based on your priorities

AI isn't just about answers. It's about *clarity* — helping you see what matters, skip the noise, and move forward with confidence.

And that clarity is what makes AI not just useful, but genuinely empowering — in your learning, your work, and your everyday decisions.

Checkpoint:

What You've Learned So Far

Before you move on, take a moment to recognize how far you've come. If you were unsure about AI when you picked up this book, you've now got a solid foundation — and that deserves a pause and a little credit.

From Curiosity to Clarity

Back in Chapter 1, you might have felt unsure about what AI actually is or how it works. Now, you understand that:

- AI isn't magic — it works by recognizing patterns

- It doesn't think or feel — but it can still be surprisingly useful

- You've already been using AI in your daily life without realizing it

You also know the difference between key types of AI:

- Generative vs. predictive

- Rule-based vs. learning-based

- Text, image, voice, and video tools — and when to use which

From Hesitation to Confidence

In Chapter 2, you explored the common fears around AI — and how to move past them. You've seen that:

- You don't need to be "technical" to get started

- Mistakes are part of learning

- AI doesn't replace your value — it supports it

Most importantly, you've started to shift from thinking, *"I don't know where to start,"* to, *"I can figure this out — step by step."*

From Information to Real-Life Use

Chapters 3 and 4 showed what AI can do for you in practical, everyday ways:

- Help with writing, summarizing, and planning

- Make personal projects more creative and fun

- Support your learning or research

- Act as a personal assistant, study partner, or quiet thought helper

You've gone beyond just knowing what AI is — you've seen how it can actually make your life easier, smoother, or more interesting.

What's Next

Now you're ready to move from learning into doing. In the next chapters, you'll:

- Choose your first AI tool

- Learn how to set it up and try it

- Practice writing simple prompts

- Avoid common beginner mistakes

You don't need to be confident yet — just open-minded and willing to explore.

Let's take that next step.

Choosing the Right AI Tools

What Makes a Good Beginner Tool

Tools That Feel Intuitive from the Start

When you're just starting out with AI, **how a tool feels to use matters just as much as what it can do**. The best beginner tools don't make you feel like you need a tutorial before you even log in — they feel natural, even if you're not entirely sure what you're doing yet.

Think of it like trying a new app on your phone. If it's friendly, clear, and you can start using it without reading the manual, you're more likely to explore and enjoy it. But if it's full of confusing menus, tiny buttons, or tech jargon, you'll probably close the tab and never go back.

What Makes a Tool Feel "Intuitive"?

Simple layout: Everything important is easy to find, and nothing feels hidden or buried under too many options.

Clear prompts or examples: Good tools often show you what to do before you even ask — like "Try asking me to summarize a document."

Immediate feedback: You get a quick result, even if it's not perfect. That feedback loop builds your confidence fast.

No pressure to "get it right": You don't have to phrase things perfectly — the tool helps you learn by doing.

How You'll Know You've Found a Good One

You'll know a beginner-friendly tool when:

- You try it once and immediately want to try it again

- You don't feel stuck or confused

- You leave the experience thinking, *"That was easier than I expected"*

The goal at this stage isn't to find the "most powerful" tool. It's to find the one that makes you feel like using AI is something you can do.

Free or Low-Cost Options to Get Started Safely

When you're just starting out with AI, you shouldn't have to spend money to see if it's right for you. Fortunately, some of the most popular and useful AI tools offer **free plans**, **trial versions**, or **limited-use tiers** that let you explore without risk.

These free or low-cost options aren't just about saving money — they also remove the pressure. You can try things, make mistakes, and experiment without worrying about wasting a subscription or committing to something too advanced.

What to Look For in a Free Plan

Not all "free" tools are equal. Here's what makes a free or low-cost plan good for beginners:

- **No credit card required to start** – You can sign up and try it without feeling locked in

- **Generous limits** – Enough daily or monthly uses to actually get a feel for how the tool works

- **Access to core features** – Even if advanced tools are behind a paywall, you should still be able to do basic tasks like writing, summarizing, or asking questions

- **Clear upgrade path** – If you do decide to go further, it should be obvious what you're paying for and why

Popular Beginner-Friendly Tools with Free Access

At the time of writing, there are many AI tools that offer useful free plans — ideal for beginners who want to explore without committing to a paid subscription. Below are some standout options, grouped loosely by purpose, so you can pick a starting point that suits your interests or needs.

Text and writing tools: Tools like **ChatGPT (Free plan with GPT-3.5)** are excellent for general writing support, brainstorming, and Q&A-style prompts. **Google Gemini (formerly Bard)** is another strong option — especially useful for planning, summarizing, and learning. For those working inside documents or note apps, **Notion AI** provides lightweight but effective writing and organization support, especially for short-form writing and task management.

Image generation tools: Canva includes free AI-powered tools that let you generate images from text prompts, remix designs, and adjust layouts quickly — even with no design experience. For more artistic or experimental imagery, platforms like **Bing Image**

Creator (powered by DALL·E) are free to try with a Microsoft account.

Video generation tools: Pika and **Runway ML** both offer free trials or limited free use for creating short AI-generated videos or enhancing clips with simple effects. These tools are beginner-accessible and can be used to generate visuals for social media, slideshows, or fun creative projects.

Voice and speech tools: ElevenLabs provides a free tier for generating lifelike voiceovers from text, which can be used for storytelling, narration, or adding voice to presentations. **Speechify** also offers a free plan for turning written content into spoken audio — useful for listening on the go or making learning more accessible.

Music and sound tools: Boomy and **Suno** are both beginner-friendly platforms that let you create music from simple prompts or templates. Boomy is great for generating full songs in various styles, while Suno lets you create catchy, vocal-led tracks with just a few lines of text. Free usage may be limited, but it's enough to explore and experiment.

Productivity and planning tools: Notion AI (mentioned above) is strong here too, as it helps turn tasks and ideas into structured notes, lists, and schedules. **ClickUp AI** also offers a free plan for task management with built-in writing and planning support for teams or individuals.

Coding and developer tools: Replit offers a free plan with access to Ghostwriter AI, which can help beginners write or understand code snippets. If you're new to coding, **ChatGPT** can also act as a tutor by explaining concepts or writing basic scripts step-by-step.

Education and study helpers: Khanmigo (by Khan Academy) and **Socratic by Google** are excellent free resources for learners. While Khanmigo may be part of a pilot program at the time of writing, Socratic is available on mobile devices and helps students understand homework problems using AI explanations. ChatGPT is also widely used by learners to ask questions, check understanding, and revise more interactively.

Marketing and business tools: Copy.ai and **Writesonic** both offer free tiers with limited credits per month, which are useful for generating product descriptions, emails, and ad copy. While they cater to marketers, beginners running side projects or small businesses can benefit from their simplicity.

Design and branding tools: Looka and **Brandmark** offer basic logo generation with free previews, perfect for individuals testing business ideas or launching personal projects. **Canva**, again, covers this space well with easy drag-and-drop tools and brand kit options even on the free plan.

You don't need to try all of these — just choose one that suits your current interest. Whether you want to write better, get organized, make music, or just explore something new, there's likely a free tool that can help you take the first step with confidence.

Tools with Built-In Help, Examples, or Active Communities

When you're trying something new, it helps to feel like you're not doing it alone. The best beginner AI tools don't just work well —

they also **show you how to use them,** offer **examples to guide your thinking,** and connect you with **other users who are asking the same questions** you are.

These kinds of support features can make the difference between feeling stuck and making progress.

What Built-In Help Looks Like

Beginner-friendly tools often come with:

- **Starter prompts** or **suggested questions** you can click on to try

- **Walkthroughs or tooltips** built into the interface

- **Templates** for common tasks like writing emails, creating lists, or designing images

- A built-in **help or search bar** that answers questions without sending you to a support page

These features remove the pressure to "figure it out" from scratch. Even if you're unsure where to begin, the tool gently nudges you forward.

Learning Through Examples

Seeing what others are doing — or what the tool itself suggests — can unlock new ideas you wouldn't have thought of on your own. Many platforms now offer:

- Prompt libraries

- Pre-built use cases

- "Inspiration galleries" (especially for visual tools like Canva or Midjourney)

- Case studies or quick start guides tailored for beginners

Even simple examples like "Ask me to summarize this email" or "Write a product description" can help spark ideas and show you what's possible.

The Value of Community

Some tools go a step further by building **active communities** where users can:

- Share prompts or ideas

- Ask beginner-level questions without judgement

- Learn from others' experiments and results

- Stay motivated by seeing what's possible

Communities like the **ChatGPT subreddit, Notion forums,** or **Canva's design community** offer extra support and make the learning curve feel a lot less steep.

When a tool includes both **functionality** and **guidance**, it doesn't just help you get results — it helps you grow more confident using AI in your own way.

Matching Tools to Your Goals

What Are You Trying to Do? (write, plan, create, learn, etc.)

Instead of asking, *"What's the best AI tool?"*, a better beginner question   is:
"What do I want help with?"

The best AI tool for you depends less on its reputation and more on your specific goal. Once you know what you want to do — even roughly — you can pick a tool that's designed to support that kind of task, and the experience will feel much smoother.

Common Goals (and How AI Can Help)

Here are some examples of everyday goals and how AI can support each one:

If you want to write: Try a tool like **ChatGPT**, **Claude**, or **Jasper** to help you draft emails, generate ideas, clean up sentences, or write creatively.

If you want to get organized or plan something: Tools like **Notion AI**, **Google Gemini**, or **ClickUp AI** can help you turn notes into lists, build outlines, or manage tasks.

If you want to create visuals or designs: Explore **Canva**, **Adobe Firefly**, or **DALL·E** for images, social posts, or presentation graphics — no design skills needed.

If you want to create videos: Try tools like **Runway ML, Pika,** or **Synthesia** to generate short clips, animated avatars, or visual scenes from simple prompts. Some tools help you edit video with AI; others generate visuals from scratch.

If you want to create music or audio: Use tools like **Boomy, Suno,** or **ElevenLabs** to experiment with sound, voice, or background music — even if you've never made music before.

If you want to learn something new: Use **ChatGPT, Khanmigo,** or **Socratic** to ask questions, get explanations, or test your understanding in plain language.

If you want to code: Platforms like **Replit Ghostwriter, GitHub Copilot,** or **ChatGPT** can help you write, understand, or improve code — even if you're just learning.

Why This Matters

You're more likely to stick with a tool if it solves a problem you actually have. Instead of feeling like you have to "learn AI," start by using it to help you do something you already care about.

When the tool fits the task, learning feels useful — not like extra work.

Picking the Right Tool Based on Your Needs

Once you have a rough idea of what you want to do — whether it's writing, learning, designing, or just experimenting — the next step is to pick a tool that's designed to help with that kind of task.

You don't need the "best" or most advanced tool — just the one that fits **what you want to try right now.**

Ask Yourself These Simple Questions

To narrow it down, try asking:

What do I want help with? (e.g. "I want to write blog posts faster" or "I want to make music for my videos")

How much time do I want to spend learning the tool? (Some tools are very beginner-friendly, others take a bit more exploring)

Do I want to keep things simple, or customize things deeply? (Some tools are plug-and-play, others give you more control)

Is the tool helping me move forward or making me feel stuck? (If it feels like a struggle from the start, it's probably not the right fit — and that's okay)

Use Case > Features

It's easy to get distracted by feature lists, but in the beginning, you don't need the tool that does everything — just the one that does **one thing well.**

For example:

Want to write better emails quickly? Start with **ChatGPT**.

Want to generate visual content for social media? Try **Canva** or **DALL·E**.

Need a video for a personal project? Explore **Pika** or **Runway ML**.

Want to create a song or backing track? Open up **Boomy** or **Suno**.

Think of it like choosing a tool in a kitchen: you wouldn't use a blender to toast bread. The "right" tool is simply the one that gets the job done — in a way that feels good to you.

A Few Starter Tool Suggestions by Use Case

If you're still not sure where to begin, here's a quick shortcut. These are all beginner-friendly tools with free access at the time of writing — each matched to a common goal:

Writing and/or Communication	Gemini
	Claude
	ChatGPT
Visual Content & Design	Canva
	Adobe Firefly
	DALL·E
Video Creation	Runway ML
	Pika
	Synthesia

Music or Sound	Suno
	Boomy
	ElevenLabs
Planning & Productivity	ClickUp AI
	Notion AI
Learning & Study Help	ChatGPT
	Socratic
	Khanmigo
Coding or Tech Skills	GitHub Copilot
	Replit Ghostwriter
Branding & Small Business	Canva
	Looka
	Brandmark

You don't need to try them all. Just pick one that lines up with what you're curious about — and give yourself permission to explore, experiment, and learn by doing.

One tool, one use case. That's all it takes to get started.

Avoiding Tool Overwhelm

How to Pick One Tool and Just Start

With so many AI tools out there — and new ones appearing every week — it's easy to fall into what's sometimes called **"choice paralysis."** You spend more time comparing options than actually trying anything. The result? You stay stuck at the starting line.

The good news is, **you don't need to find the perfect tool. You just need one that works well enough to help you begin.**

Here's a Simple Way to Decide:

1. **Go back to your goal.** What do you want help with right now — writing something, organizing ideas, creating a visual?

2. **Choose a tool that supports that one goal.** Ignore features you don't need yet. Don't worry about what's most popular. Just find a tool that helps with *your* task.

3. **Try it once.** Not with pressure. Not with the expectation of getting a perfect result. Just test it out and see how it feels.

4. **Give yourself permission to learn as you go.** The first try is just a starting point. You'll get more confident with every attempt.

A Helpful Reminder:

You're not making a lifetime commitment. You're not choosing a tool to use forever. You're just choosing a tool to explore — today.

Progress doesn't start with the perfect tool. It starts with *any* tool — and a willingness to try it.

Red Flags to Watch Out For (Complexity, Cost, Privacy)

Not all AI tools are beginner-friendly — and not all "free" tools are as free as they seem. When you're exploring new options, it helps to know what to watch out for so you don't waste time, get discouraged, or accidentally share more than you intended.

Here are a few common red flags to keep an eye on.

1. Overly Complex Interfaces

If a tool is filled with buttons, menus, and jargon you don't understand — and it doesn't guide you through what to do — it might not be the right fit for now. Even if it's powerful, it's not helpful if it makes you feel lost.

Look for tools that feel welcoming from the first screen, not ones that expect you to already know what you're doing.

2. Hidden or Confusing Pricing

Some tools advertise themselves as free, but once you sign up, you realize:

- You only get 3 uses a month

- The features you actually need are locked behind a paywall

- You're asked for a credit card up front, even for a "free trial"

That doesn't mean paid tools are bad — but as a beginner, it's best to **start with tools that let you explore without financial pressure.**

3. Privacy Concerns or Vague Data Policies

Before you upload personal information, sensitive documents, or images, take a quick look at the tool's privacy policy (or help section).

Ask yourself:

- Does this tool store or learn from what I enter?

- Can I delete my data easily?

- Does it explain clearly what happens to my content?

If the answers aren't clear — or if something feels off — it's okay to walk away. Trustworthy tools are upfront about how they handle your data.

AI tools should make you feel more in control, not less. If a tool feels confusing, pushy, or secretive, it's a sign to pause and reassess.

How to Grow Your Toolkit Over Time Without Burning Out

It's tempting, once you start to see what AI can do, to want to try everything at once. There are tools for writing, tools for designing, tools for planning, tools that make music, videos, voices—and all of them promise to save you time or unlock your creativity.

But growth doesn't happen by chasing every tool. It happens by going deeper with the ones that actually help you.

Start with one or two tools that feel useful or fun. Give yourself space to explore, mess around, and figure out what you like about them. Once those feel natural, you can start to notice gaps. Maybe you love using ChatGPT for writing, but wish you had something visual for design. That's when it makes sense to add something like Canva or DALL·E.

Over time, your toolkit becomes personal. Not based on what's popular, but on what genuinely supports how you think, create, and learn. Some people end up using five or six tools regularly. Others stick to just one and get incredible value from it. There's no right answer.

What matters most is that the tools fit *you*—not the other way around.

Your First Steps with AI

Setting Up Your First AI Account

You've explored what AI is, what it can do, and how to find a tool that fits your goals. Now it's time to stop reading *about* AI and start actually *using* it. This chapter is all about helping you get started — practically, confidently, and at your own pace.

What You'll Need (Email, Browser, Device Basics)

Setting up your first AI account doesn't require any special tech skills — if you've ever signed up for an email, streaming service, or social media account, you already know what to do.

Here's what you'll need to get started:

An email address – Most tools will ask you to sign up using an email (or connect through Google, Apple, or Microsoft). If you already have a personal email address you use regularly, that's enough.

A web browser – Tools like ChatGPT, Gemini, and Canva work directly in your browser. You don't need to install anything. Chrome, Safari, Edge, or Firefox will all do the job.

A basic device – Most tools work fine on a laptop, desktop, or tablet. Some even run well on phones, though a larger screen often makes things easier when you're just starting out. You don't need a powerful machine — just something modern enough to run a browser smoothly.

A stable internet connection – Because most AI tools run online (they don't live on your computer), you'll need to be connected. Slow internet might make things feel sluggish, but for most beginner tasks, even a modest connection will do.

There's no need to overthink this. You likely already have everything required. The goal is to take the pressure off. You're not setting up a complex software system — you're just opening a door. And the simplest setup is enough to walk through it.

Creating a Secure Login and Keeping Your Data Safe

Signing up for an AI tool is usually quick and easy — just enter your email, create a password, and you're in. But even at this early stage, it's worth thinking about **security and privacy**. You're not doing anything risky, but like with any online service, it helps to start with good habits.

Use a Strong Password (Or a Password Manager)

Choose a password that's hard to guess — not your pet's name or your favorite band. If you're using a tool you might return to often (like ChatGPT or Notion), it's worth storing your password safely in a password manager like 1Password or Bitwarden.

If the tool allows two-factor authentication (2FA), turn it on. It adds an extra layer of security and only takes a few seconds.

Be Mindful of What You Share

AI tools like ChatGPT don't "remember" personal conversations unless you're logged in — and even then, the data may be used to train the model unless you adjust your settings.

That means you shouldn't enter:

- Passwords or sensitive personal information

- Bank details or private client data

- Anything you wouldn't be comfortable sharing with a support team

Think of the AI as a helpful assistant — smart, but not private by default.

Check the Settings

Most tools have a basic settings panel where you can:

- Turn off chat history or data sharing (if available)

- Choose whether your prompts are stored

- Review what data is collected

You don't have to obsess over privacy, but being aware of what you're agreeing to puts you in control — and that's what this journey is all about.

When you treat your login like you would for online banking or email, you set yourself up to explore AI tools confidently, without second-guessing what's happening behind the scenes.

Exploring the Dashboard or Interface with Curiosity

Once you've signed in, you'll land on the tool's main dashboard — or what some call the "home screen" or "workspace." This is where you'll interact with the AI, type your prompts, see your results, and navigate any extra features.

If you're new to all this, it's completely normal to feel unsure of what to click on. So instead of trying to memorize everything or use it "correctly," just treat this first visit like you're exploring a new room. Look around. Press a few buttons. See what happens.

You're not going to break anything.

What You'll Usually See

Different tools look slightly different, but most beginner-friendly platforms share some common elements:

A text box or chat area where you can type your request

A sidebar with past conversations, templates, or saved content

Menu options for settings, help, or account info

Examples or suggestions to help you get started ("Try asking me to write an email")

Many tools — especially writing or chatbot-style platforms — are designed to feel like a friendly conversation. You don't have to use perfect grammar or technical terms. Just type how you naturally speak.

Curiosity Is More Important Than Confidence

There's no one right way to explore an AI tool. If you see a button you don't recognize, click it. If there's a sample prompt, try it. If something confuses you, ask the AI to explain what it does.

The best way to learn is by playing.

You don't have to master the layout in one sitting. You just have to get familiar enough to know where to start next time.

Making Your First Prompt or Request

What a Prompt Is, in Real Terms

The word "prompt" can sound technical or intimidating at first — like something you need to write perfectly or structure in a special way. But in real terms, a prompt is just **a message, request, or question you type into the AI**.

It's you talking to the tool.

If you've ever typed something into Google, sent a text message, or asked Siri or Alexa a question, you've already used prompts — you just didn't call them that.

Think of It Like This:

A prompt is how you **start the conversation** with an AI tool. It's your way of saying:

"Here's what I need help with — can you help me?"

That could be:

"Summarize this article in plain English."

"Write a polite response to this email."

"Give me dinner ideas using rice and eggs."

"Help me plan a two-day trip to Edinburgh."

"Explain quantum physics like I'm five."

You don't have to worry about getting the words just right. The AI is built to understand natural language — so just say what you mean, and it'll do its best to help.

The best way to understand prompts is to try one. You don't need a perfect question. You just need to ask.

Step-by-Step: Writing Your First Prompt and Refining the Results

Now that you know a prompt is just a question or request, it's time to actually try one. This section isn't about getting it "right" — it's about building confidence by seeing how flexible and forgiving AI tools really are.

Let's walk through the process, one step at a time.

Step 1: Think of Something Simple You'd Like Help With

Pick something small and useful — something you might ask a friend or search engine. For example:

"Write a friendly message to say I'll be late to dinner."

"Give me three gift ideas for someone who likes gardening."

"Explain how credit cards work in basic terms."

Choose something that feels relevant to your life — that way, the response is more meaningful and easier to judge.

Step 2: Type It in Naturally

Go to the text box, and type your request like you're talking to a helpful person:

"Can you write a short thank-you note for a neighbor who brought me soup when I was sick?"

No need for formal phrasing or keywords. Just speak human.

Step 3: Read the Response — Then Reflect

The AI will usually reply within a few seconds. Read through it. Ask yourself:

- Does this sound right to me?

- Is the tone too formal? Too casual?

- Does it include the details I want?

It's okay if it's not perfect — this is where refinement comes in.

Step 4: Refine the Prompt to Get Closer to What You Want

This is the real secret to using AI effectively: **don't stop at the first result.** If it's not quite right, just keep talking.

Try things like:

"Make it sound more casual."

"Add a sentence about how I appreciated the flowers too."

"Can you shorten it to two sentences?"

"Write a version I could say out loud, not in a card."

Each adjustment helps the tool learn what you're looking for — and helps *you* learn how to guide it more clearly.

This back-and-forth is normal, and it's where the learning happens. The more you try, the faster you'll figure out how to shape prompts to get exactly what you need — and you'll be amazed how quickly it starts to feel natural.

Examples of How a Small Change in Wording Changes the Outcome

One of the most helpful things to learn early on is that AI responds not just to *what* you ask, but *how* you ask it. Even small changes in the tone, focus, or structure of your prompt can shift the result in surprisingly effective ways.

Let's look at a real example. Each of the prompts below asked ChatGPT about the benefits of walking every day — but with a slightly different instruction. Here's how those changes affected the outcome.

Prompt: *Write a short paragraph about the benefits of walking every day.*

Response: Walking every day offers a wide range of physical and mental health benefits. It improves cardiovascular fitness, strengthens muscles and bones, and helps maintain a healthy weight. Regular walking can also reduce the risk of chronic conditions like heart disease, type 2 diabetes, and high blood pressure. Beyond physical health, daily walks boost mood, reduce stress, and enhance mental clarity by promoting the release of endorphins. It's a simple, low-impact activity that can be easily incorporated into any routine, making it an accessible way to support long-term well-being.

This is a well-rounded, informative answer — perfect if you're looking for a general overview.

Prompt: *Write a short, upbeat paragraph about the benefits of walking every day.*

Response: Walking every day is a simple habit with powerful benefits! Just a short stroll can boost your energy, clear your mind, and lift your mood. It gets your heart pumping, strengthens your body, and helps keep stress at bay. Plus, it's a great way to enjoy fresh air, explore your surroundings, and take a break from screens. Whether it's a quick morning walk or an evening unwind, daily walking is a feel-good step toward better health and happiness.

This time, the tone shifts noticeably — it's more cheerful and energetic, with an encouraging voice that feels almost promotional.

Prompt: *Write a short paragraph I could say to a friend to convince them to start walking every day.*

Response: Honestly, you should try walking every day—it makes such a difference. Even just 20 minutes can boost your mood, clear your head, and give you more energy. It's such an easy way to feel better, get a bit of exercise, and take a break from everything. Plus, it adds up over time—you'll feel stronger, sleep better, and it's actually a nice way to unwind. Want to start together?

Here the tone becomes casual and conversational — like real dialogue. It's no longer an informative paragraph; it's a suggestion made in a relatable voice.

Prompt: *Write a short paragraph explaining the benefits of walking every day to a teenager.*

Response: Walking every day might not sound exciting, but it actually has a ton of benefits. It helps clear your mind, boosts your energy, and even improves your mood—kind of like a reset button when you're stressed or tired. It's also great for your body, keeping your heart healthy and your muscles active without needing a gym. You can listen to music, catch up on podcasts, or just enjoy being outside. It's an easy way to feel better, think more clearly, and stay healthy without overthinking it.

The language here is simplified and relatable — still informative, but now styled for a younger reader who might need the "why" to feel personal or cool.

Prompt: *Write a paragraph about how daily walking can help with mental health and stress.*

Response: Daily walking is a powerful way to support your mental health and reduce stress. The steady rhythm of walking helps calm the nervous system, clear your mind, and release built-up tension. It boosts the production of endorphins—natural mood lifters that help you feel more positive and relaxed. Whether you're dealing with anxiety, feeling overwhelmed, or just need a mental break, a walk can create space to breathe, reflect, and reset. Over time, this simple habit can lead to greater emotional resilience and a more balanced mindset.

This version doesn't talk about general health at all — it focuses entirely on emotional well-being, just as the prompt asked.

Prompt: *List three quick bullet points about why walking every day is helpful.*

Response:

- Boosts mood and reduces stress by releasing feel-good endorphins.

- Improves physical health by strengthening the heart, muscles, and joints.

- Increases energy and focus by improving circulation and clearing the mind.

This one's all about formatting. The same content is still there, but the style makes it easier to skim or use in notes, lists, or slides.

You don't need to memorize these changes or get every word right. The point is to see how small adjustments to your prompt — tone, format, audience, or focus — help shape the outcome. It's a conversation, not a command. And the more you experiment, the better you'll get at making the AI work for you.

Common Mistakes Beginners Make (and How to Avoid Them)

Expecting Perfect Results on the First Try

One of the most common early missteps with AI is assuming that whatever it gives you on the first try is either **exactly right** or **completely wrong**. If it's not perfect, many people think, *"This doesn't work"* — and give up.

But the truth is, the first result is rarely the final one. Think of it like getting a rough draft from a very fast assistant. You're still part of the process. The role of the AI is to get things started quickly — not to magically guess your ideal answer without guidance.

It's more helpful to approach the first response as a starting point — something to react to. If it's too long, ask the AI to shorten it. If the tone feels off, tell it to try again with a different style. If it missed part of what you needed, just add a bit more context and rerun it.

In time, you'll come to see that the *real power* of AI isn't in getting it right instantly — it's in how fast it can adapt when you steer it. That back-and-forth is part of the design, not a sign of failure.

Giving Up After One Weird or Wrong Answer

Almost everyone who tries AI for the first time has a moment when the tool gives a strange or disappointing answer. It might sound robotic, completely miss the point, or just feel… off. That can be frustrating, especially if you were expecting something smart and seamless. But here's the truth: weird answers are part of the process — not the end of it.

What often happens is this: someone types a prompt, gets a confusing or useless reply, and assumes the tool just doesn't work. But in most cases, the issue isn't the tool — it's that the prompt didn't give quite enough information, or that the AI made a guess that missed the mark.

This is where a simple mindset shift makes all the difference. Instead of giving up, you keep going. You tweak the request. You rephrase the question. You give the AI a little more to work with.

You might say something like, "That's not quite what I meant — try again but make it shorter," or "Focus more on the stress relief part," or "Can you say it in a friendlier tone?" That kind of feedback is what AI tools are designed for. The more you steer, the better the results become.

Don't expect perfection on the first try. Expect a rough start that you can refine. If the first answer is strange or off, that's normal. What matters is what you do next.

Not Exploring or Tweaking Enough to Learn What's Possible

A common beginner mistake isn't using the tool *wrong* — it's simply not using it *enough*. Many people try one or two prompts, get a decent result, and stop there. They never realize how much more powerful the tool becomes when you start exploring and tweaking.

The real strength of AI lies in its adaptability. You can ask it to:

Rewrite something in a more casual or professional tone

Shorten a long explanation into a bullet-point list

Expand a summary into a full article

Explain a complex idea in simple terms

Reword something for a different audience, like kids or clients

Turn plain text into a social media post, a headline, or a story

These aren't tricks. They're everyday ways to teach the tool what you want — and to teach yourself what's possible.

The more you adjust and experiment, the more you begin to see AI not just as a novelty, but as a creative partner. You stop thinking of it as a one-shot question box, and start using it like a flexible engine that responds to your direction.

If your early prompts gave decent results, that's a great start. But the next step — the real growth — comes from pushing beyond decent. Try new angles. Tweak what worked. Ask the same question in a different way.

Curiosity is the key that unlocks what AI can truly do. If you keep turning that key, you'll find new possibilities every time.

Using AI to Support Your Daily Life

AI doesn't have to be saved for big tasks or creative projects. Some of its most useful applications are the smallest — the kind you can build into your daily habits. From reminders and reflections to mental resets and planning, AI can quietly support your routines behind the scenes, helping your day run more smoothly with very little effort.

Building Simple Daily Routines with AI

Morning Check-Ins for Planning, Journaling, Mindset

A short check-in with an AI tool in the morning can set the tone for the entire day. It's like having a quick conversation with a thoughtful assistant — one who's ready to help you focus, organize, and reflect before the day gets away from you.

You might start with something simple:

"Help me list my top three priorities today."

"Give me a one-line affirmation for focus and calm."

"Turn this to-do list into a timeline I can follow."

"What's a good journaling prompt for self-awareness today?"

These quick prompts take less than a few seconds to write, and the replies you get can serve as gentle nudges — not just for productivity, but for mindset. You can also ask the AI to help you break down a busy day, reorder your tasks by urgency, or offer ideas for how to handle something that feels overwhelming.

And if your morning routine includes writing, journaling, or intention-setting, AI can act as a thought partner, helping you reflect with clarity. You might say:

"Ask me a journaling question about gratitude."

"Help me reframe this anxious thought more positively."

"Suggest a mindful intention I can carry into the day."

It's a light, low-pressure way to begin with focus — and it can shift your whole experience of the hours ahead.

Using AI for Meal Ideas, Reminders, Affirmations, or Motivation

AI can also play a small but useful role in the everyday tasks that often drain your energy — like figuring out what to eat, remembering errands, or trying to stay mentally on track during a busy week.

You don't need a dedicated app for each of these things. One simple AI tool can help with all of them — especially when you approach it with the same tone you'd use when asking a friend.

Here are a few examples:

For meal ideas

"Give me three quick dinner ideas using eggs, spinach, and cheese."

"What can I make in under 15 minutes with no oven?"

"Suggest a healthy lunch for someone who works from home."

For gentle reminders

"List out the three things I can't forget to do today."

"Help me create a short checklist for packing my bag tonight."

"Turn this list into a schedule I can follow in 30-minute blocks."

For affirmations or motivation

"Write a calming affirmation for someone who feels behind."

"Give me a short mantra for staying focused and not comparing myself to others."

"Help me start the day with a confident, grounded mindset."

The beauty of using AI this way is that it meets you where you are. If your brain feels scattered, it can help pull things into order. If you're tired or unmotivated, it can offer just enough structure or encouragement to help you move forward.

You don't need to use it every day. But knowing it's there — ready to support the small things that often get overlooked — can take just enough pressure off your shoulders to make a difference.

Making Your Day Smoother with Small, Supportive Prompts

Some of the most effective uses of AI are also the simplest. A single sentence at the right moment can save time, reduce stress, or give you a clearer headspace. These aren't dramatic changes — just quiet nudges that make daily life a little easier to navigate.

Think of these small prompts as mental shortcuts. When you're overwhelmed, distracted, or just feeling a bit stuck, they can help you pause, reset, or regain focus without needing to dive into a complex system or app.

Here are a few types of micro-support that can fit into your day:

Mental reset:

"What's one small thing I can do to feel less overwhelmed right now?"

Clarity check:

"Help me summarize what I'm trying to get done this afternoon."

Energy shift:

"Suggest a two-minute breathing exercise or mini break idea."

Framing the day:

"Write a gentle reminder that it's okay to move at my own pace."

The point isn't to become dependent on AI to tell you what to do. It's to use it as a sounding board — a second brain you can lean on for clarity, especially when your own feels full.

Once you start using AI this way, it becomes part of the rhythm of your day. Not a big, dramatic tool. Just something quietly useful that helps things flow.

Making Work Tasks Easier (Even If You're Not in an "AI Job")

You don't need to work in tech, marketing, or data science to benefit from AI. In fact, many of the most useful applications are for people in completely non-digital roles — small business owners, teachers, freelancers, admin staff, or anyone juggling multiple responsibilities.

What makes AI so helpful at work isn't its complexity — it's its ability to take everyday tasks and make them quicker, smoother, or less stressful. You don't need to use it all day. Just using it for ten minutes to handle something repetitive can make a real difference.

Writing Emails, Reports, or Summaries Faster

Writing is one of the biggest time drains in any job. Whether it's composing polite emails, explaining something clearly, or condensing information for someone else, most people spend far more time writing than they realize.

This is where AI can quietly save hours.

Let's say you need to write an email but you're tired, distracted, or not sure how to start. Instead of staring at a blank screen, you could try:

"Write a polite email reminding someone to send a document by Friday."

"Turn this list into a short summary I can paste into a report."

"Help me explain this project update in plain English."

"Draft a follow-up message for someone I met at a networking event."

AI can give you a starting point in seconds. You can then adjust the tone, change the details, or ask it to rewrite the message to sound more like you.

Even for longer writing tasks, such as summarizing meeting notes or turning rough bullet points into a report draft, it can take the mental load off and help you move from scattered thoughts to structured output — quickly and without fuss.

You're still in control of the final wording. But you're no longer starting from scratch. And that's often the hardest part.

Outlining Presentations or Documents with Ease

Starting from a blank page is one of the biggest creative hurdles in any job — especially when you're expected to put together a report, slide deck, article, or proposal on short notice. You might know what you want to say, but turning scattered ideas into a clear, structured outline can take more time than writing the content itself.

AI tools are especially helpful at this early stage. With just a sentence or two, you can generate a framework that gets you moving. It won't be perfect, but it will save you from the hardest part: starting.

Here are a few simple ways to prompt an outline:

"Give me a basic structure for a 10-minute presentation on eco-friendly packaging."

"Help me organize my points for a blog post about remote team productivity."

"Turn these notes into a report outline I can expand later."

"What are the typical sections in a proposal to pitch a new service?"

The results won't be polished, but they give you something to react to. You can then reorder, remove, or add detail based on your needs — much faster than building the structure from scratch.

If you're working on something longer, like a workshop, course, or client brief, AI can help you break it into manageable sections. It can also suggest headings, offer title options, or help you condense a long idea into a one-page summary.

The key benefit isn't just speed — it's the mental relief of not having to do all the structuring alone.

Brainstorming or Simplifying Tasks in Your Own Voice

Not everything at work comes with a clear starting point. Sometimes the real challenge is figuring out how to frame an idea, explain something simply, or untangle the noise in your own head. It's not that you don't know what to do — you just can't quite see the path clearly yet.

This is where AI becomes surprisingly helpful. You're not asking it to write for you. You're using it to think alongside you.

You might begin with something like:

"I've got these three ideas, but I'm not sure how to combine them into a plan."
Or:

"I know what I want to say, but it's a mess in my head — help me sort it out."

From there, the tool responds. It gives you a rough version of the thing you were trying to build — not finished, not perfect, but structured. Something you can react to. And that reaction, that instinctive "yes, but…" or "no, more like this," is where real clarity starts.

Sometimes you'll ask it to rewrite what you've said in simpler language. Other times you'll have it organize your thoughts into steps, or explain your idea as if it were being pitched to someone else.

What's powerful here isn't just the output — it's what the process unlocks. The moment you see your vague thoughts reflected back in sentences, paragraphs, or next steps, your brain stops spinning and starts responding. You move from *I don't know how to say this* to *that's close — now let's improve it.*

You're still in control. You're still the voice behind the message. But now you've got a second brain that's not tired, not blocked, and not overthinking it.

Supporting Personal Projects and Hobbies

AI isn't just for productivity or work. Some of its most satisfying uses come when you apply it to personal projects — things that bring joy, creativity, or a sense of progress in your own life. Whether you're making something for fun, planning an event, or just adding a thoughtful touch to your day, AI can offer just enough help to spark ideas or save time, without taking over the creative part you actually enjoy.

Creating Posts, Cards, Invites, or Captions

Let's say you're putting together a birthday invite, a thank-you card, or a social media post — something small, personal, and ideally well-worded. That's exactly the kind of moment where AI can quietly step in, clean things up, or give you a stronger starting point.

You might write a rough message like: *"Hey, we're doing a picnic for Emma's birthday — bring snacks, come early if you can."* Then ask the AI: *"Can you turn this into a fun invite for a group text or Instagram post?"*

In seconds, it gives you a version that keeps your tone but smooths it out. It might add warmth, polish the phrasing, or suggest a punchy caption that sounds like you — just slightly more confident and clearer.

Or maybe you're making a thank-you card and want something sweet but not cheesy. You can say, *"Write a short message to thank someone who helped me during a really tough week — I want it to feel personal but not overly emotional."*

The tool responds with something balanced — heartfelt without being heavy, personal without being overdone. You can tweak a word or two and call it done.

What you're doing here isn't outsourcing creativity. You're using AI as a collaborator — the kind who helps you find just the right words when you're short on time or mental energy. And when it works, it's quietly satisfying. Not dramatic, just helpful.

Planning Holidays, Events, or DIY Projects

Planning something fun should feel exciting — but more often than not, it starts with overwhelm. Where do you begin? What should you include? How do you keep it simple without missing something important?

This is where AI can step in, not to take control, but to give you structure.

Let's say you're thinking about a weekend trip. You could start with something as casual as: *"I want to take a two-day break in the countryside. Help me sketch out a plan that's relaxing, not too expensive, and doesn't involve too much driving."* From there, the AI can suggest a basic itinerary, ideas for meals, and even throw in reminders like packing lists or travel tips.

Planning a party or family gathering? You might say, *"Help me plan a small birthday lunch for 10 people, with ideas for food, timing, and a backup plan if it rains."* Instead of trawling through dozens of articles or Pinterest boards, you get a tailored answer in seconds — something you can adjust and build on.

Even DIY projects can benefit. Not sure where to start with a home improvement idea or crafting experiment? Try, *"Give me a simple step-by-step plan to paint and decorate a hallway wall using things I can buy locally."* The AI won't swing a hammer for you, but it will break down the tasks and flag details you might not have considered.

In all of these cases, what you're really getting is a shortcut to clarity. You supply the intention, and the AI gives you a shape —

something to react to, refine, or run with. That's what makes it so helpful: it supports the plan without replacing the person behind it.

Using AI to Learn Something New, Without Pressure

Learning something new as an adult often comes with hidden resistance — not because you can't do it, but because it feels like there's too much to know and not enough time to learn it properly. The idea of starting a new skill from scratch can trigger pressure, self-doubt, or the nagging feeling that you're already behind.

This is where AI can quietly shift the experience. It removes the formality of a class or course and replaces it with conversation — one where you set the pace, ask the questions, and steer the direction.

You might begin with something broad: *"I've always wanted to learn how to draw. Where should I start if I only have 20 minutes a day?"* The AI responds with a gentle entry point — nothing intimidating, just a few steps to get going. And if the suggestions don't quite fit your style or schedule, you can ask it to adjust: *"Make it even simpler,"* or *"Suggest ways to make it more fun."*

The same works for languages, photography, gardening, budgeting — any area where the first step is simply knowing what the first step should be.

What makes this different from a search engine is the adaptability. If you don't understand something, you don't have to click through five articles. You just ask: *"Can you explain that again, but more simply?"* And if you're curious about taking it further, the tool can suggest resources, routines, or small practice exercises based on what you've said you enjoy.

There's no pressure. No grades. Just a safe space to explore something you're curious about, on your terms. And often, that's all you need to turn "someday" into "I started."

Building Confidence and Staying Current

By now, you've seen that AI isn't just for experts or big tech companies. It's for everyday use — whether you're planning your day, tackling work tasks, or exploring personal interests. But one thing that still holds many people back is confidence. Not confidence in the tool — confidence in themselves, in knowing they're "doing it right."

This chapter is about building that confidence, gently and sustainably, so that using AI becomes second nature — not something you second-guess.

Developing Your AI Confidence

Celebrate Small Wins - Even Weird Outputs Teach Something

Every interaction with AI is a learning moment, even when the result is unexpected. You might prompt it to summarize an email, and it rewrites it in overly formal language. Or you ask for dinner ideas and it includes ingredients you don't have. These aren't failures — they're feedback.

When the AI gives you something that feels "off," that's your opportunity to clarify, redirect, or refine. You're not doing it wrong — you're participating in the process. And every time you rephrase a prompt or ask for a better version, you're building both skill and fluency.

Instead of measuring success only by perfect results, start noticing progress in smaller ways: You tried a prompt you wouldn't have

written last week. You recognized what didn't sound like you —
and fixed it. You went back and asked for a rewrite instead of giving
up.

These are small wins. Stack enough of them together, and they
build real confidence. The kind that lets you say, "I don't need to
know everything — I just need to know how to keep going."

Why Repetition Builds Skill, Not Boredom

At first, using AI might feel like a novelty — a fun tool you try out
here and there. But like anything you want to get better at, skill
comes through doing it more than once. Repeating the process
doesn't just build familiarity. It builds fluency.

Every time you try a new prompt — even if it's similar to one
you've used before — you learn something. You notice what
phrasing works better. You start spotting patterns in the way the
AI responds. You naturally refine your language, become more
precise in what you ask for, and gain a sense of how to guide the
tool toward a better result.

This isn't boring. It's practice — the kind that turns guesswork into
instinct.

Think about how you learned to write emails, drive a car, or cook
something without a recipe. The first few times required thought,
maybe even hesitation. But over time, you didn't just remember
how to do it — you stopped worrying about whether you were
doing it right.

That's exactly what happens with AI. The more you use it in everyday moments, the less you overthink it, and the more confident you become.

You don't need to "study" AI. You just need to use it often enough that asking for help, adjusting a result, or trying again starts to feel normal — not like a test you might fail.

Join Communities to Ask Questions, Share Prompts, or Learn Tricks

One of the easiest ways to build your confidence with AI — especially when you're not sure if you're "doing it right" — is to spend a little time around other people who are learning too. You don't have to become a forum junkie or follow every AI trend online, but finding one or two communities where people are openly sharing prompts, asking questions, or talking through problems can quietly accelerate your growth.

You might come across someone using AI in a way you hadn't considered — like simplifying a complex contract, outlining a recipe book, or using it to draft gentle reminders for themselves. You'll also see examples of prompts that get surprisingly good results, and others that don't work at all. Both are useful.

Most importantly, you realize you're not alone in the learning curve.

Good communities aren't filled with experts showing off. They're made up of regular people trying things, sharing what worked, and asking the kinds of questions you didn't know you were allowed to ask.

You can start by searching terms like *"ChatGPT beginner tips"* or *"AI prompt sharing"* on Reddit, YouTube, or in Facebook groups. Some tools even have their own built-in user spaces — like Canva's forums or Notion's help boards.

The goal isn't to collect more information. It's to stay connected to others who are figuring it out too. When you do that, confidence stops being a solo project — and becomes something that grows more naturally, almost by osmosis.

Staying Safe and Responsible

The Difference Between Being Curious and Over-Reliant

The more you use AI, the easier it is to lean on it. And while there's nothing wrong with that — after all, it's a tool designed to help — it's important to remember the balance. Curiosity is what moves you forward. Over-reliance is what can quietly narrow your thinking.

If you find yourself running every small decision through the AI, or deferring to its answer even when it doesn't feel right, it might be time to pause. The tool is fast, but it's not always wise. And it doesn't know *you* — your values, your judgement, your experience — unless you remain actively involved in the process.

One of the best ways to stay grounded is to regularly ask yourself, *"Do I understand what this answer means?"* or *"Does this match how I'd normally think or speak?"* If the answer is no, that's your cue to step back and reassess. Curiosity leads to better thinking. But critical thinking — your own — has to stay in the driver's seat.

Spotting AI Hallucinations or Mistakes

AI tools can sound incredibly confident — even when they're completely wrong.

This is known as an *hallucination*: when the AI invents facts, misrepresents information, or fills in gaps with something that sounds plausible but isn't accurate. It doesn't do this on purpose. It's not trying to trick you. It simply doesn't "know" things the way humans do — it generates responses based on patterns in language, not verified knowledge.

You might ask for a summary of a book, and it invents a character that doesn't exist. Or request a list of historical events, and it includes a made-up date. Often, it sounds completely believable — which is what makes it so easy to trust without checking.

Here's the simple rule: **if accuracy matters, double-check.** If you're writing a blog post, citing a quote, listing statistics, or making a business decision — always verify anything that sounds like a fact. Use a search engine. Look up the source. Or better yet, ask the AI to provide a reference and see if it holds up.

Even in casual use, it's helpful to get in the habit of gently questioning what you're reading. Not with suspicion — just with curiosity. Does this sound right? Would I say it this way? Is this the kind of thing I could actually verify?

When you approach AI with a light layer of awareness — not fear, just attention — you keep your judgement sharp, and your outcomes trustworthy.

Protecting Your Privacy Without Compromising Curiosity

One of the smartest things you can do as a beginner is get comfortable using AI — while also knowing where to draw the line. Curiosity is essential. But so is protecting your personal data, your digital footprint, and your peace of mind.

You don't need to be paranoid. You just need to be aware of what you're sharing — and how the tool handles it.

As a general rule, avoid entering anything you wouldn't put in an email to a stranger. That means no bank details, home addresses, private logins, or sensitive client information. Even if the tool says it's private, you're still communicating with a system that stores and processes your input, at least temporarily.

That said, you can stay curious and still stay safe. When experimenting, use placeholders like "X Company" instead of real names, or describe the situation instead of copying and pasting actual documents. If a tool offers a privacy toggle or lets you turn off data training, use it. And if you're unsure, check the tool's help or settings panel — most platforms now offer clear explanations of what they do (or don't) store.

Learning to use AI responsibly isn't about fear — it's about ownership. You get to decide how much you share, what feels appropriate, and how to work with the tool in a way that protects both your ideas and your identity.

You can be curious, creative, and in control — all at the same time.

What's Next on Your AI Journey

Choosing Where to Go Deeper Based on What You Enjoy

By this point, you've done more than just "try AI." You've explored how it works, how to shape prompts, how to use it in daily life — and most importantly, how to make it your own.

Now comes the fun part: deciding where to take it next.

There's no right path forward. Some people find themselves using AI to support their creative side — writing stories, planning events, experimenting with design. Others lean into productivity and organization, streamlining work tasks or planning smarter days. Some discover a love of structured thinking and go deeper into automation, code, or business applications.

The key is to notice what's been most useful or interesting to you so far. Where did you feel most engaged? When did time pass quickly? Which tasks felt easier — or more fun — with AI in the mix?

Instead of thinking, *"What should I learn next?"* ask, *"What do I want to try more of?"*

Your curiosity is the compass. Whether it leads you deeper into a niche or just wider into new kinds of experimentation, you'll make progress faster — and enjoy the process more — by following what already resonates.

Areas to Explore: Creative Writing, Productivity Hacks, Even Coding

Once you've built confidence using AI for everyday tasks, you might feel ready to explore something a little more focused — not because you *have* to, but because certain areas start to feel more intriguing or rewarding.

If you've enjoyed playing with language, AI can be a great tool for creative writing. You can co-write poems, short stories, song lyrics, or dialogue scenes. You can also use it to outline a novel, explore character ideas, or turn a rough journal entry into something more expressive. The tool doesn't replace your voice — it reflects it, nudges it forward, and sometimes shows you unexpected paths.

Maybe you're drawn more to structure than storytelling. In that case, AI shines when it comes to productivity. You can explore how to automate your day with task lists, convert your goals into weekly check-ins, or even ask the AI to act as a coach, holding you accountable with daily summaries or reflection prompts. It's less about hacks, more about flow — finding little ways to make each part of your day smoother and more intentional.

And then there's coding. If you've ever been curious but intimidated by the idea of learning to code, this is one of the most powerful entry points available. You can ask basic questions, get real-time feedback, and learn through conversation — rather than memorization. Tools like ChatGPT, Replit Ghostwriter, and GitHub Copilot can guide you through projects step by step, helping you build scripts, websites, or automations even if you're starting from zero.

Whether you lean toward the creative, the practical, or the technical, AI doesn't force you to pick a lane. It simply meets you where your curiosity goes — and helps you move forward with less friction.

Final Thoughts

If you've made it this far, you've already done more than most. You've stepped beyond the headlines and hype, explored how AI actually works, and tried using it in ways that fit your life — not someone else's agenda.

This book wasn't written to make you an expert. It was written to give you a clear path from *curious but unsure* to *confident and capable*. And now that you've reached the end, here's the truth:

You're already capable.

You don't need to know everything about how AI works behind the scenes. You just need to keep asking good questions, trying things out, and learning as you go. Every weird response, every small success, every moment of friction — it's all part of building fluency. AI isn't a finish line. It's a tool. And now it's one you know how to use.

If there's one takeaway to carry forward, let it be this: You don't have to become someone else to use AI well. You just have to bring more of yourself to the process — your voice, your context, your goals — and let the tool meet you there.

From here, the journey's yours. Keep exploring. Keep tweaking. And most importantly, keep creating.

You're not late. You're right on time.

Appendix:

Resources to Keep Learning

As you continue to explore AI, here are some hand-picked resources to help you learn more, try new tools, and stay up to date — at your own pace.

Recommended Books

The Art of Prompt Engineering with ChatGPT by Nathan Hunter
A practical, hands-on guide to writing better prompts and improving your results.

You Look Like a Thing and I Love You by Janelle Shane
A witty, accessible introduction to how AI works (and why it sometimes gets things hilariously wrong).

The AI Engineer's Toolkit by Louis Bouchard
A simple breakdown of how AI models work, how prompting fits in, and what's coming next.

Beginner-Friendly YouTube Channels

Matt Wolfe
Clear weekly videos exploring the newest AI tools and how to use them.

What's AI
Explainer videos and visual breakdowns of core AI concepts.

Simpletivity
Tips and walkthroughs for using AI tools in everyday productivity.

Useful Newsletters

The Rundown AI
Quick summaries of tools, tips, and trends.

Ben's Bites
Daily AI news with a light tone and practical focus.

Import AI by Jack Clark
Thoughtful essays and links covering the broader AI landscape.

AI Tool Report
Tool reviews and beginner use cases.

AI Tools Mentioned in This Book

ChatGPT – General-purpose conversational AI.

Google Gemini – Planning and search-focused chatbot (formerly Bard).

Claude – Friendly and capable language model by Anthropic.

Poe – Access and test multiple AI models in one place.

Notion AI – AI-powered planning, writing, and content support.

Grok (by xAI) – A conversational AI chatbot developed by Elon Musk's company, xAI.

Canva AI – Design and image generation built into Canva's visual platform.

Adobe Firefly – AI features for creatives and designers.

DALL·E – Create images from text prompts (by OpenAI).

Runway ML – AI-powered video, image, and motion design tools.

Pika – Generate short-form AI video content from text.

Synthesia – Create talking-head videos from scripts.

Suno – Turn text prompts into full-length music tracks.

Udio – Advanced AI music composition.

Boomy – Beginner-friendly music creation platform.

ElevenLabs – High-quality text-to-speech with custom voices.

ClickUp AI – Task and productivity support inside ClickUp.

Socratic – Google's AI learning assistant for students.

Khanmigo – AI tutor and learning assistant from Khan Academy.

Replit Ghostwriter – Real-time coding assistant built into Replit.

GitHub Copilot – AI-powered code suggestions inside your editor.

Looka – Logo and branding generator using AI.

Brandmark – Design brand visuals and logos with AI support.

Printed in Dunstable, United Kingdom

66902065R00077